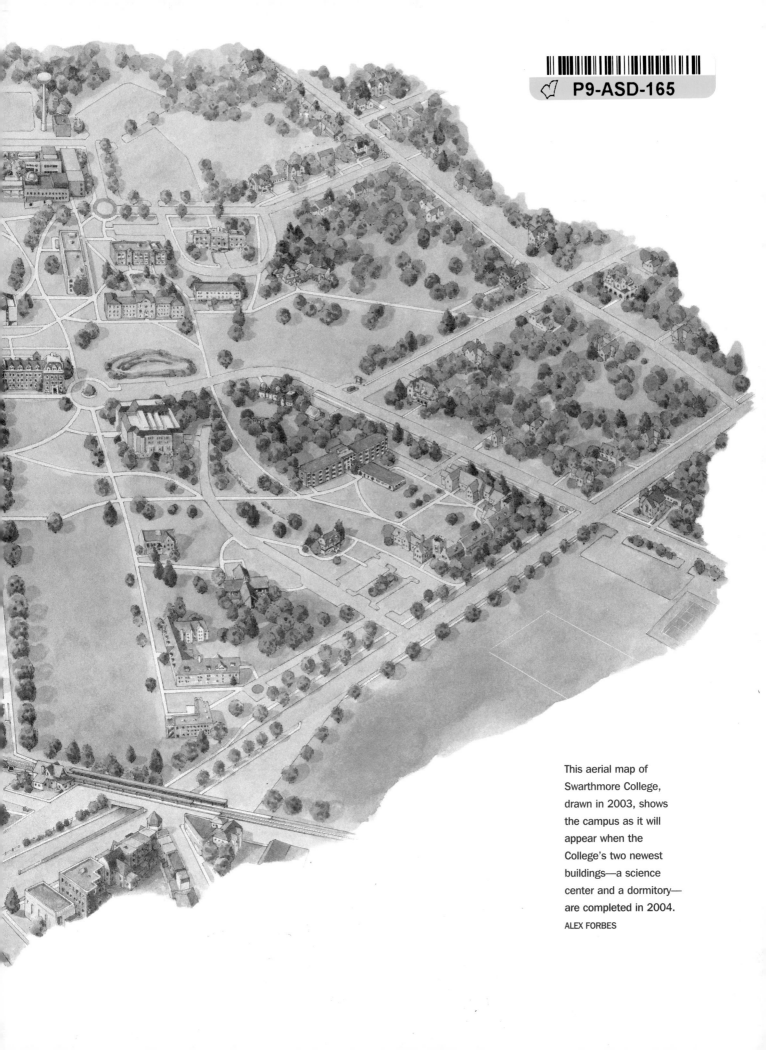

P9-ASD-165

This aerial map of Swarthmore College, drawn in 2003, shows the campus as it will appear when the College's two newest buildings—a science center and a dormitory—are completed in 2004.

ALEX FORBES

Salute to The Scott Arboretum

The 75th anniversary of The Scott Arboretum is of great interest to State Street Corporation. We have enjoyed watching and helping Swarthmore College since 1982. We know how important the arboretum has been to several generations of Swarthmore students and alumni.

The Scott Arboretum educates, inspires, calms, reassures, and entertains. Its many visitors have come away awed by its beauty, diversity, and design. It has become an outstanding national institution of horticultural excellence, accompanying Swarthmore College, which occupies a similar reputation in U.S. higher education.

State Street is proud to join in supporting The Scott Arboretum and Swarthmore College by sponsoring this limited-edition publication to commemorate and help support Scott's mission of conservation, education, recreation, and science. We congratulate the staff and volunteers and patrons of the arboretum on a wonderful book and on 75 years of bringing the wonders of nature to generations in the Delaware Valley and those from around the country—and even from abroad.

George Russell Jr.
Executive Vice President and Director
Global Philanthropy Program
State Street Corporation
225 Franklin Street
Boston MA 02110

Acknowledgment

The Scott Arboretum and Swarthmore College gratefully acknowledge the grant of $55,000 given by State Street Corporation of Boston in April 2000, which has made possible the publication of this 75th-anniversary book.

Alfred H. Bloom
President of Swarthmore College

Claire Sawyers
Director of The Scott Arboretum

THE
DONNING COMPANY
PUBLISHERS

THE SCOTT ARBORETUM
OF SWARTHMORE COLLEGE
The First 75 Years

by Ben Yagoda

The Donning Company Publishers
184 Business Park Drive, Suite 206
Virginia Beach VA 23462

Library of Congress Cataloging-in-Publication Data

Yagoda, Ben.
　　The Scott Arboretum of Swarthmore College : the first 75 years /
　　by Ben Yagoda.
　　　　p. cm.
　　ISBN 1–57864–207–8
　　　1. Swarthmore College. Scott Arboretum—History. I. Title.

QK480.U52S368 2003
580'.7'374814—dc21

　　　　　　　　　　　　　　　　　　2003041034

Printed in the United States of America on recycled paper.

The paper used in this publication meets the minimum requirements of
ANSI/NISO Z39.48–1992 (R 1997) (Permanence of Paper).

Dust Jacket:

Front: The Dean Bond
Rose Garden at the
height of summer bloom.
(Photo taken ca. 1990.)
GOTTLIEB HAMPFLER

Back: The Scott
Arboretum offices as
seen from the Terry
Shane Teaching Garden.
HARRY KALISH

Title Pages:

Left: Specimen trees are
one of the trademarks of
the arboretum-campus.
(Photo taken 1992.)
THE TERRY WILD STUDIO

Right: The Scott Outdoor
Amphitheater in autumn
colors. (Photo taken 2000.)
HARRY KALISH

Contents

Director's Note

My dream to create this book in celebration of The Scott Arboretum's 75th anniversary would not have been realized without the contributions of some talented and generous individuals. Special thanks go to George Russell Jr., the director of the Global Philanthropy Program at State Street Corporation, who looked favorably on our proposal to produce this book; and to Dan West, vice president for alumni, development, and public relations at Swarthmore

HARRY KALISH

College, who believed in the arboretum and this project enough to present our proposal. Thanks also to Martha Meier Dean '71, former director of development, who also devoted energy to that effort.

Thanks to these individuals who served on the steering committee at the beginning of the project and assisted in selecting a wonderful author: Martha Dean, Kathy Grace, Jeff Lott, Susanna Morikawa, Barbara Haddad Ryan '59, and Larry Schall '75. I deeply appreciate the work of Ben Yagoda, who wove together the history of the arboretum without the benefit of organized archives or a support staff. T. Kaori Kitao was willing to share with us her unique ability to see the arboretum and campus development from a profound viewpoint. My thanks also go to those who reviewed material along the way: Maralyn Orbison Gillespie '49; Anne Bonner; Dan West; and arboretum staff members; to Jeff Lott and the Publications Office staff for tying up lots of details at the end; and to those at The Donning Company who showed us the way to share and celebrate the history of The Scott Arboretum in this book.

Claire Sawyers
Director of The Scott Arboretum

Author's Note

The principal written sources for this book were the annual reports of The Scott Foundation (later The Scott Arboretum); *Hybrid* (a newsletter published quarterly by the Associates of The Scott Arboretum); and clippings, manuscripts, correspondence, memoranda, and other documents in The Scott Foundation papers and presidential papers in the Friends Historical Library of Swarthmore College. Photographs not credited are courtesy of the archives of The Scott Arboretum or Friends Historical Library of Swarthmore College. I would like to make special mention of the interviews with Anne Wood and John and Gertrude Wister conducted by Jane Pepper in the 1970s, the transcripts of which are in the Friends Historical Library. I conducted interviews with Andrew Bunting, Michael Claffey, James Duell, William Frederick '48, Maralyn Orbison Gillespie '49, Josephine Hopkins, Jeff Jabco, Mark Jacobs, James Janczewski, Julie Jenney, Kendall Landis '48, Roger Latham '83, Rhoda Maurer, David Melrose, Allison Necaise, Joseph Oppe, Greg Paige, Claire Sawyers, Larry Schall '75, Sue Schmidt, Barbara Seymour '63, Terry Shane, Suzanne Welsh, and Judith Zuk. Letters from Donna Edwards, Quentin Weaver, and the late John Nason were helpful. I would like to thank Jeff Lott, director of publications at Swarthmore College and his staff, and Susanna Morikawa, archivist of the Friends Historical Library, for their assistance and support. Thanks also to Claire Sawyers, who had the idea for this book and whose knowledge, efficiency, and consideration made it a pleasure to write.

Ben Yagoda

Introduction

Oaks and Organizations

By Claire Sawyers, director of The Scott Arboretum

Oaks and organizations. Planting an oak tree and creating an organization are acts that symbolize our confidence in the future. We trust both will live well beyond us. As decades pass, the seedling becomes a tree, and the fledgling organization reaches its own maturity. Then, it can become easy to take both big oaks and active organizations for granted. Surely, we slip into thinking, they will always be there—nature or inertia will take care of them.

But gardeners know it takes more than hope and luck for an oak tree to survive. A tree may require watering during droughts and protection from predators both large and microscopic—and from change and development around it. Some trees need lightning rods to protect them from strikes, pruning of dead wood, or the removal of encroaching weeds—to name just a few ways a mature tree may need our help.

So it is with organizations. The creation of The Scott Foundation on June 3, 1929, was both an act of hope and remembrance. This memorial to Arthur Hoyt Scott on the campus he loved has grown deep roots in the landscape of Swarthmore College, making it one of the most beautiful in America. The Scott Arboretum, as it is now called, has counted on countless gardeners to envision, finance, care for, and protect it. During the past 75 years, its leaders, workers, and volunteers have made it possible for all of us to enjoy this beauty around us.

A postcard, postmarked in 1912, of the swamp white oaks.

8

This book celebrates the history and legacy of The Scott Arboretum as it marks its 75th anniversary. But beyond the celebration, this story, by chronicling the development of the arboretum, illustrates how organizations take more than hope and luck to thrive. Thus, the book is as much about the future as it is about the past.

I invite you to savor the beauty of the arboretum captured in these photographs while discovering in its story the generosity and hard work that—along with a lot of hope and no small amount of luck—have seen this organization to its current vitality. With an increased awareness and newfound appreciation of the efforts it took from those who have gone before me, this milestone prompts me to also encourage you to contribute actively to the growth, protection, and nurturing of The Scott Arboretum, along with its oaks, if you want it to be a part of the landscape of the future.

The bender oak (*Quercus x benderi*) is thought to be about 300 years old, the oldest tree on campus. Sadly, it lost several lower limbs to storms in the 1990s.

Foreword

Arboretum, Landscape, and the College

By T. Kaori Kitao, William R. Kenan Jr., Professor Emerita of Art History

I interviewed for a teaching position at Swarthmore College in 1966. I flew in one Saturday morning in January, a bright sunny day after a heavy snow, and recall vividly the white splendor of the campus. After a series of relentless interviews that lasted the whole day, I told myself that, if it were offered, I would take the job—no matter what positive or negative conditions might exist. In my naïveté, I had no knowledge of Swarthmore's reputation as a superb liberal arts college until I started teaching here. But I saw the beauty of the campus with my own eyes.

It was not until late in May that I returned to Swarthmore to serve as an honors examiner. The campus looked completely different, still beautiful but not as stunning as it had looked in the snow that January morning. It was only late in the second semester of my first teaching year, during spring 1967, that I witnessed in awe the succession of resplendent blossoms, starting with forsythia and crocuses and continuing all the way to the roses fully ready for commencement.

I was told on the day of my interview that the Swarthmore campus is an arboretum. No doubt, I was told, too, of the then Scott Foundation. A few years passed before I became aware of the foundation's presence and its work, but I was always appreciative of the campus—every one of the 35 years that I was in service to the college. Having lived many of these years in one of the faculty houses on campus, I could easily delude myself that the whole campus was my personal garden, maintained by a mysterious team of gardeners who would come and go whenever they were needed.

So, having retired in 2001, I feel especially nostalgic as I write this foreword, which I was kindly invited to contribute to this commemorative book about The Scott Arboretum. This work completes a full circle. I have been given the opportunity to contemplate the beauty of the campus all over again.

The importance of The Scott Arboretum to Swarthmore College is undeniable, but it is never obvious and can be easily ignored. The college does not offer courses in horticulture. Botany is a subject in the Biology Department. No curriculum exists in landscape design either. The potential of the arboretum's plant collections as teaching resources, therefore, has remained largely unexplored—or, at best, underused— perhaps with the exception of the Crum Woods, which has served the environmental studies curriculum more recently. Students walk by the plant specimens, but by and large, they ignore them. Some, no doubt, take note of the flowers in bloom—who can resist spring blossoms? But few stop to read the tags on the trees, shrubs, and flower beds, and even fewer understand their meaning.

Americans are avid gardeners, even among city dwellers. This interest is largely the result of English heritage in the American culture. Thomas Jefferson designed his dwelling, Monticello, as a working farm, following the model of the English gentry of his century. This tradition dies hard; it also accounts for the overriding national aspiration for country living and continuous exodus of the upwardly mobile to the suburbs, exurbs, and beyond.

Conversely, since Roman Antiquity, Europeans have lived in apartment houses in urban centers unless they were farmers. They still do. It is not only Venice that is treeless; cities may have parks and boulevards planted with trees, but private gardens are for the rich exclusively. Yet for Americans, house and garden are inseparable. It's the house and the garden together that make a home.

The student population of Swarthmore College comes predominantly from suburban homes. But with the exception of the few students who fill their dormitory rooms with potted plants and eagerly work for the arboretum, they are not gardeners. Lack of time alone does not keep this number small, although schoolwork and social activities occupy students while they live on campus. Most are indifferent because, for the most part, horticulture is beyond the realm of their immediate interest. Enthusiasm for gardening does not begin until some years after their graduation, when they become homeowners. In the four years they spend at the college, students remain largely oblivious to the arboretum's valuable plant collections.

So, on the surface, the benefit to the college of the arboretum's influence on its grounds is largely cosmetic. Planting embellishes the landscape to befit the college's suburban setting—another Jeffersonian heritage. Just as he chose a farm as his personal residence, Jefferson deemed the University of Virginia as his institution of higher learning, similarly sited away from the city to protect impressionable young minds from city vices.

The pastoral ideal shaped college planning in America. If our students are oblivious to horticulture, they are never unaware of the pastoral setting that the grounds' caretakers assure them. Every student remembers Swarthmore as a beautiful place—not just the Scott Outdoor Amphitheater, which students love and experience vividly as the site of their commencement. The enduring value of a beautiful setting can easily slip out of the consciousness of those who reside here yearly; even if the college does not make use of the arboretum academically, it absorbs its lushness by osmosis.

The arboretum provides an idyllic setting for the college. But, in reality, it does more; it not only embellishes but also edifies. This result is not immediately apparent, but it is the nature of a landscape that teaches without trying. No planting here happens haphazardly. The whole idea of plant collections organizes the campus into clusters of memorable places. We remember different parts of the campus by the plants that distinguish them: a grove of lilacs, patches of tree peonies, the rose garden, a lawn surrounded by cherries, magnolias here, hydrangeas there, and so forth. These places might even have gained a literary aura had they been given evocative names identifying them as special places, as was done in the garden of the Katsura Palace in Kyoto or Hadrian's Villa at Tivoli. Landscape gains its shape from the memory it stirs in our mind.

Plant collections, as opposed to random or mixed planting, automatically organize space that would otherwise be amorphous and allow us to organize the campus visually—to orient ourselves. Each collection possesses a distinct identity that endows it with a sense of place, even without poetic names attached to it. Some people always walk around blindfolded, but when we "read" the landscape, we are training ourselves to perceive space more accurately. Modest as it may seem, plant collections contribute to the education of sight. In this respect, horticultural partitioning of the ground, if done wisely, is superior to any mediocre effort at landscaping. It is not the plant material per se, but the way it is arranged and composed that makes a good landscape. Every planting is an act of design. Each new tree or shrub positioned in a certain way defines the spatial configuration in its domain.

It is exceedingly fortunate that the Swarthmore campus lies on a hillside, which provides a variety of terrains. It offers many potentially interesting spatial entities, or "capabilities," as would have said the 18th-century English landscape designer Lancelot "Capability" Brown, in reference to which he received his moniker. Thus, we have the panoramic view from Parrish Hall, the embracing basin surrounded by cherry trees, an extended vista, a meandering path, a little enclave here, an enclosure there. The Scott Arboretum did not create these capabilities, but its conscious design has generated paths of remarkable variety, rich in rise and fall, shifting perspectives, changing spatial configurations, now narrowing and now spreading out, a long stretch followed by a pregnant pause, and, too, varying light conditions, now bright, somber, open, shaded, and mottled.

One of the most satisfying visual and spatial sequences is the path I call the President's Stroll, which goes from Parrish Hall's rear portico toward Trotter Hall, past Pearson Hall and the Swarthmore Friends Meetinghouse; then along the wooded path and out to the open lawn; and, finally, over to shaded Cedar Lane, leading to the Courtney Smith House, the president's residence. The sequence is as satisfying tracing the path backward to Parrish. The spatial-kinesthetic sequence of such a walk is best described as choreographic. As a linear sequence, like music, it is articulated temporally by stretches and leaps and pauses; spatially, it is characterized by expansion and contraction and deflections. The passage from Worth Health Center up toward the McCabe Library terrace to Kohlberg Hall provides a similar varied sequence. Magill Walk is a straight path reinforced by the rows of oak trees, screening without closing it off, and we are drawn to the focal point of Parrish Hall. But those who are willing will see and appreciate, when they come to the steps, how the Parrish porch sinks out of view for part of the climb, then rises again like a ship on the horizon.

In my opinion, the campus nevertheless has a generous share of ill-articulated or unarticulated spaces and sequences; I call them "vagues." There is little to impress us in the vagues, however embellished they may be with pretty plants. Overplanting is one sure way to blur and disarticulate a space; overscaling is another. We can't remember vagues clearly because they form blanks in our memory. One example of a vague—emphasizing, by contrast, the virtues of the President's Stroll—is the downhill path from Parrish to Sharples Dining Hall, which is notably weak in articulation. From the top, the view is open and undifferentiated, with Sharples lying low in the distance like a crouching tortoise. The passage uphill, which I have facetiously christened the Eaton Run, is arduous—not just because the stomach is full and the uphill incline steep but, more important, because it is monotonously uniform in its rise and feels interminable.

Of course, vagues can be useful; they offer nice challenges to the arboretum. The college's well-articulated passages, including the trails in the Crum Woods, not only provide us with a rich visual experience but, often unbeknownst to us, sharpen our sensitivity to the spatial environment. No reason exists for us not to have more of them and eliminate vagues. Designers of Japanese stroll gardens developed such an art to perfection. A good landscape edifies.

Physically, Swarthmore College today sits on The Scott Arboretum. But historically, the arboretum was constructed around the campus architecture. The college was founded in 1864 and its main building completed in 1869 (it was not called Parrish Hall until 1902). It is reported that, at the time, there were "but two trees" on the entire tract. Early photographs show us how incredibly bare it was in those years. As we read in this book, Arthur Hoyt Scott, Class of 1895, planted 100 lilacs in 1915 "to beautify the Swarthmore campus." He first envisioned an arboretum on the college campus in the mid-1920s. But it was only in 1931 that President Frank Aydelotte approved the proposal, and John Wister (H'42) was appointed director of The Arthur Hoyt Scott Horticultural Foundation. He served in that capacity until 1969. With the assistance of Superintendent of Building and Grounds Harry Wood's knowledge of English gardening, Wister was largely responsible for shaping the basic visual character of the arboretum-campus. But its development was slow.

The history of The Scott Foundation informs us of the inordinate resistance of the college administration to the arboretum project and Wister's self-sacrificing dedication to its cause. Wister was a shy person who lacked political influence to inspire the college to do more for him and for the arboretum. Shortage of funds and manpower were his perpetual obstacles to maintaining the collections, not to speak of realizing his own ambitious ideas as well as those of Scott. Yet, viewed in a larger cultural context, I believe the problem was greater than his limited rhetorical prowess and meager budget. It ran much deeper.

For a college aspiring to rise in intellectual superiority under the stewardship of President Aydelotte—who reinvented Swarthmore with his visionary Honors Program in the 1920s—horticulture was a pleasant but inessential accessory and a low priority. The college collectively must have seen horticulture as distinctly subservient to academic pursuits. It was a cosmetic, and embellishment was a frivolous pursuit. Moreover, because gardening engages the hands, it was thought to lack intellectual rigor to serve the college in any significant degree. Gardening is gardening. No one, of course, put it quite this way; however, the underlying sense, unstated but universally understood, was a cultural code of the time, to put it in semiotic terms. This code, in fact, prevailed throughout the professions of architecture and landscape architecture in America.

Until quite recently, architects tended to consider landscape design secondary in importance and subordinate to their own discipline. Students in architecture who were not doing well were often channeled to landscape architecture, even though presumably they had no greater success there if they hadn't succeeded in architecture. In campus planning, it was once customary to retain an architect to design and construct a new building; after that project was complete, a landscape designer, or a nursery person in some scenarios, was hired. He (only rarely she) would fill up the space outside the new building with vegetation to soften its silhouette and provide a pleasant setting—in short, to embellish it. Architecture was stone and mortar; landscape architecture was vegetation, soft as opposed to hard and mutable versus enduring. The situation is changing in these professions, if still slowly. Better architects work with their landscape colleagues from early in the planning stage, recognizing that buildings and gardens that complement each other create a more satisfying overall environmental design. Yet the old hierarchy is deeply rooted in the everyday understanding of what the garden is in the Anglo-American tradition. It is most essentially planting—trees, shrubs, and flowers—arranged around the house to embellish it, like a necklace and a hat to frame the face. It is an appendage separate from the house rather than its extension or an integral part of it.

Nature and humanity are on equal terms rather than at odds with each other in Japan and certain other non-Western cultures. But in the strain of the Platonic dualism, so persistent in the West, nature is subordinate to humanity. Even in 18th-century England's so-called natural gardens, the country estate would have a garden modeled after nature to accentuate the rational order of its architectural construction. Jefferson's Monticello dominated the land it occupied. Parrish Hall, which was the college when it was founded, similarly sat on the hilltop, surveying the campus as its overlord. So the college's garden, developed only years later, may have been considered desirable but remained subservient to the built structures.

By the same token, those who professed the tending of this garden did not quite enjoy the status of the college's professors and administrators. Work that engages the hands can never reach the height of the work of the intellect—so the thinking went.

The prevailing prejudice continues to linger. As recently as 1982, the college rejected the recommendation of a visiting committee to accord the director of the arboretum a faculty status or its equivalent, possibly "with some teaching responsibility."

Only when we set Swarthmore in this cultural context do we understand—indeed, with much sympathy—Frank Aydelotte's resistance to the grand vision of Scott and Wister. Only then, too, do we realize the greatness of Wister's monumental contribution, not to speak of the depth of his conviction and persistence. He was a landscape designer trained at Harvard, shortly after it had established the country's first degree program in the subject. But he was a distinguished horticulturist, with deep interest in plants since his youth. So, the focus of his efforts, in my understanding, was consistently plant collections. His ambitious scheme for the main campus was to arrange plants "grouped according to their botanical family." The spaces they defined were secondary in his consideration. Collections were also the subject of the wide acclaim he received through the 1930s. As late as 1945, his arboretum was praised for "a floral display." Yet Wister managed to achieve happy results in spatial design. He knew landscape architecture. But it must be noted that, to his advantage, space was then abundant. It is no longer so.

For most of its history, greenery defined the character of the Swarthmore campus. Foliage, like the mist over the human habitation in Zen landscape paintings, unified the campus at one time by washing over the scattered buildings. But this is no longer true, at least for the north campus, which is the more highly trafficked section of the college and therefore the part that we experience most acutely each day. Three buildings (McCabe Library, Sharples Dining Hall, and DuPont Science Building) were relatively new when I arrived in Swarthmore in 1966. During my 35 years of service to the college, at least two new buildings were built each decade, occupying new sites on the campus. More are still to come. Swarthmore is still a wooded campus in comparison with any urban one, and greenery still shrouds its peripheries. At one time, nevertheless, Martin Biology Building stood in the open, and the view down from Parrish was a vast expanse.

The campus, once pastoral, has become suburban. It was spacious when I arrived in 1966, and in my early years, I observed that the college's buildings didn't form a community because they turned their backs on each other and failed to converse. Today, they are beginning to sit closely together as in a crowded waiting room. I don't bewail these changes in the least; building up is surely a sign of prosperity. For many years, siting a new building started by identifying available open spaces on campus and choosing one so that each new building would be an isolated entity. This process is readily seen in the self-sufficient Sharples, McCabe, Trotter, DuPont (at the time of its building), and Mertz, among others. Each developed its own landscape, much like a house with its own lot and property lines. The possibility that a new building might be constructed adjacent to the existing one, or even tangent with it, often eluded the early planners.

In recent years, however, we have seen significant changes in both physical planning and landscape design. I am happy to observe that newer buildings are sited in clusters, close together, not only to achieve greater integration and cohesion as a community but also—and significantly—to preserve the ever-diminishing open spaces on the campus. In addition, these new buildings have incorporated landscaping as a necessary part of the building design. The north campus is evolving into an inter-locked complex of buildings and enclosed landscaped areas. This new development is also bringing to the arboretum a twofold challenge.

By its very nature, The Scott Arboretum has been from the beginning horticultural in its basic mission and, therefore, in its thinking and practice. Quite rightly, it continues to be so.

Over the years, its interest and concern have inevitably focused on planting in general and plant collections in particular. The arboretum-campus has, therefore, developed by piecemeal additions as building projects arose without a truly viable master plan. The architectural activities of recent decades, especially the latest one, have created a new mission for the arboretum. Buildings are not only crowding in and usurping campus land. Because the spaces between buildings are no longer as ample as they used to be, planting—once an activity totally in the domain of the natural environment (as opposed to physical construction)—is now part of the physical planning. The college and arboretum must now work together to design planting not so much around buildings but between them, requiring the arboretum staff to think at once like horticulturists and landscape designers.

In my years at Swarthmore, I have seen the arboretum make spectacular growth thanks to the able leadership of succeeding directors: Joe Oppe; Judy Zuk; and, currently, Claire Sawyers. It has met one of the central missions of the foundation as initially conceived by Scott: the horticultural education of the public and the college community. The Scott Arboretum now offers extensive and varied public programs and publications. It has also been meeting its new mission of developing well-designed gardens. Now, we have not only the superb Terry Shane Teaching Garden but also many recognizably defined areas of planting, often linked to specific buildings. The Isabelle Bennett Cosby ['28] Courtyard is an example, serving not only Kohlberg Hall but also embellishing Parrish Hall. The campus has become so much richer, especially in the last decade.

But as with older campus buildings, these gardens are often entities unto them-selves and therefore self-isolating. The Scott Arboretum at its 75th year is perhaps ready to meet its second great challenge: In collaboration with future college planners and builders, it must look at a larger picture—the whole campus as an integral compo-sition. The arboretum-campus in the current state still suffers from fragmentation. More attention must be given to creating smoother links among designed entities, both buildings and gardens. By links, I don't necessarily mean walks and footpaths but, most of all, nodes, vistas, and inflections (such as pacing, rhythm, suspense, and other means of articulations), elements of spatial design that establish continuities, contrasts, and transitions. Of all the parties who make decisions about the college's future, the arboretum is the one that knows how and can do this best.

Planting a single tree is an act of design that defines the surrounding space and has the capacity to establish visual and spatial axes and links. A visitor walking up the path from Benjamin West House, for example, encounters a spectacular oblique view of Parrish Hall; this asset, in my view, remains underappreciated. Similarly, the link between Kohlberg Hall and McCabe Library might be strengthened with a vista rather than obscured with planting. A well-acted play makes the story unfold naturally and does not tax the spectator to resort to reading the synopsis. A well-designed landscape is similarly self-explanatory visually, spatially, and ideologically.

A momentous event in the history of The Scott Arboretum occurred in March 1995, virtually unnoticed by the college community at large: The arboretum was granted accreditation by the American Association of Museums. This national recognition, which is given to fewer than 750 of the nation's 8,500 museums, validates the arboretum's intellectual foundation and accords it the status of a professional institution. It is evidence not only of the well-earned achievement of the arboretum but also of the more enthusiastic support it has been receiving from the college in recent decades.

A further concerted effort between the two institutions, I trust, should bring about closer integrated intellectual programs in the college curriculum. Harvard has the Arnold Arboretum, but it is on a separate ground; the Morris Arboretum is across the town from the University of Pennsylvania. Only at Swarthmore is the campus itself the arboretum. This situation is unusual—an arrangement that invites a whole range of imaginative teaching that is not easily feasible elsewhere. The arboretum can and should teach not only area garden enthusiasts but the students of Swarthmore College itself.

I am aiming high, of course—for which I may be faulted. But who would have imagined, in my first years of teaching at this college, that studio art, together with performance arts, would become a vital part of Swarthmore education that they are today?

As striking as the campus was in my first encounter, I am fully aware that it is even more beautiful today. But I also believe that it can be still better. The sprawling campus can be an articulately structured composition, like a well-designed novel or a play, and serve as the model pastoral-suburban campus commensurate with Swarthmore's reputation in academic excellence. We can then all celebrate the arboretum-campus as an integral part of the liberal arts education at Swarthmore.

Spring
A Day in the Life of The Scott Arboretum

A bright Tuesday morning, late April. After a chilly early spring, the Philadelphia area has been zapped by a brief but powerful heat wave; the temperature reached 90 degrees yesterday, and the same is expected for today. On the Swarthmore College campus, the college's various constituencies prepare for the business of the morning: Students begin trickling in to their carrels at McCabe Library, professors to their classrooms, administrators to their offices. The outfit of choice is sandals, T-shirts, and shorts.

The thermometer reading is atypical, but in one way, this morning is like most: Few of the people walking by take a moment to look up and absorb what is around them. If they did, they would see a single day's chapter in a year-round novel. Today, what's most visible is a kind of transition of blossoms, with dogwood trees just beginning to bloom, cherry and crabapple trees and viburnum bushes near their flowery peak, and magnolias and daffodils already starting to fade.

The Chinese Terrace graced by the early spring blooms of the Chinese magnolia or saucer magnolia (Magnolia x soulangiana). (Photo taken 1993.)
CLAIRE SAWYERS

Nature is the principal playwright of this procession, but on Swarthmore's 325 acres, it has a local dramaturge: The Scott Arboretum. Indeed, the entire campus is an arboretum and has been since 1929. Every day, the campus is host to schoolkids, horticultural professionals, garden-club enthusiasts, and local strollers who have come to examine or simply enjoy the collection. When they look closely, they would see that every tree and shrub on campus has a metal dog tag attached to it, identifying its scientific name and accession number. Detailed descriptive brochures are there for the taking in weather-proof boxes adjacent to a dozen or so of the most notable collections. In all, some 10,920 woody plants, representing more than 3,000 different taxa, are in the collection. No one has attempted to count up the total number of herbaceous plants; it would be a thankless and probably impossible task.

The holly collection, which contains more than 320 different types of holly, was donated by James Frorer '15 in 1974. It remains one of the arboretum's significant collections today. (Photo taken 1998.)

One factor in the occasional obliviousness of Swarthmore students, no doubt, is that despite the palpable beauty and world-renowned collections of roses, hollies, rhododendrons, lilacs, and tree peonies that thrive outside their classroom and dormitory windows, the dominant aesthetic here—as the foregoing list might indicate—eschews the dramatic and exotic for a kind of heightened vision of the everyday. Even on a spectacular morning like today, instead of overwhelming you, it sneaks up. This effect is in keeping with the arboretum's mandate. It was started in 1929, two years after the death of its namesake, Arthur Hoyt Scott, a captain of industry. Scott was an enthusiastic gardener, especially known for his work with irises and peonies, and he believed in the gospel of gardening—one not yet universally embraced, in those pre–Martha Stewart days. His widow and some relatives and friends established the arboretum in his memory and according to his philosophy. As an early statement in the 1932 *Swarthmore College Bulletin* put it: "The founders have wished to make possible a dream of Mr. Scott's to help horticulture by visual demonstration. They have believed that this dream can be realized by planting in a public place of such trees, shrubs, and flowers as can be used by people of average means living in the Philadelphia suburban area. While they wish this planting to be of scientific value, they have no wish to duplicate the work of existing botanical gardens, which already cover their field well. Rather they wish this to be a practical horticultural garden. The term 'practical' may be defined as referring to plants hardy, without special care in the climate of Eastern Pennsylvania."

Yellow magnolias blooming in early spring at the base of Clothier Tower. (Photo taken 2003.)

The arboretum has grown exponentially since then and, truth to tell, has dabbled in the exotic, but it has remained true to its mission. Its work is overseen in Cunningham House, a compact, shingled dwelling next to McCabe Library and its headquarters since 1971. Surrounded by perennial gardens that, in this springtime moment, seem to be inching up before your eyes, it has a small pool, sometimes stocked with fish, in the back. If you take a careful look, you will notice that one wing of the building is topped by a dome; the reason is that, until 1911, this was the site of the college's astronomic observatory.

The office won't officially open till 8:30 a.m., 15 minutes from now, but already activities are in progress. One of the arboretum's big events of the year, Arbor Day, is only five days away, and Allison Necaise, the assistant education coordinator, is on her way to a nursery in Chester County, about 15 miles away, to pick up tree seedlings that will be given away to all who ask for them. She ends up with two kinds—trident maple and giant arborvitae.

The Suzanne Schmidt Memorial Garden, located in the cherry collection, includes sweeps of bulbs, daylilies, and ferns. The garden is dedicated to Suzanne Boissard Schmidt '46, a longtime Scott Associate. (Photo taken 1998.)
CLAIRE SAWYERS

Soon after the doors open, some early arrivals among today's crop of volunteers are having coffee, munching on cookies and strawberries, and chatting in the bright room set aside for them. The Arboretum Assistants Program has been in place since 1987 and is, in retrospect, a brilliant idea. The assistants, of which there are currently about 100, get invaluable training in horticultural techniques and information—itself in keeping with the arboretum's educational mandate—plus a sense of belonging to and helping an important community resource, not to mention free cookies. The Scott Arboretum gets free labor—which is the main reason it has been able, since the late 1980s, to expand dramatically its collections of herbaceous flowers, which are undeniably lovely but notoriously labor intensive. Today, with the need to get the campus looking its best for Arbor Day, a comparatively large contingent of 18 volunteers will eventually report for duties ranging from putting labels on plants, to stuffing envelopes for mailings, to (the largest category) doing actual gardening work in the collections.

By a couple of minutes past 9 a.m., eight volunteers in floppy hats are gathered outside the front door. They will be divided into two groups: Greg Paige, who has the somewhat unwieldy title of integrated pest monitor and volunteer coordinator, leads one; Sue Stark, whose position is, simply and rather elegantly, gardener, coordinates the other. "You have two wonderful choices," Greg tells them. "You can go to the Cherry Border and do some weeding, and what else?" He looks at Sue.

"Weeding," Sue says.

"Which area has more shade?" a female volunteer asks. Not surprisingly, given the requirement to be available to work on weekdays, she, like many if not most of the volunteers, is retired or of retirement age. It already feels like 85 degrees in the sun, so the question is not merely of academic interest.

But Greg is no help; he says it's a toss-up.

The Terry Shane Teaching Garden shortly after its completion. (Photo taken 1990.)

The lilac collection today features about 80 select cultivars of the genus Syringa. *(Photo taken 2000.)*
HARRY KALISH

The volunteers duly divide themselves into one group of four and one of five; each is issued a bucket, a kneeling pad, and a hand hoe. The quartet makes its way to the Cherry Border, along Cedar Lane; the others go down the hill to the Summer Bloom Border, a bed next to the Benjamin West House that needs some final cleanup work before mulching. Forty percent of the crew are Bob '56 and Nony Barr. Shortly after Bob retired as Swarthmore's dean of admissions in 1996, they moved into a condominium near the campus and thereby lost their garden. Ever since then, the Barrs have been Scott volunteers. Pushing a wheelbarrow filled with tools down the hill, Bob says that although Swarthmore students may not seem to pay much attention to the arboretum and may not know the whys and wherefores of its mission and function, they do appreciate the beauty it brings to their environment. "We used to do a postenrollment survey of freshmen every fall, where we asked them to rank the reasons they chose to come to Swarthmore," he says. "The attractiveness of the campus was always in the top three or four."

At the garden, Greg points out which growths are to be weeded out and which ones are to stay. "The ivy goes—the motto is, 'Ivy free by 2003.'" He points to a series of small plants. "Leave that blue plant. It's in here every year, and every year we ask ourselves, 'What is it?'" Bob asks about another shoot, back behind a bush. As Greg answers, Bob whispers, "This is called volunteer stall." Even so, within minutes, all four volunteers are hard at work. By 9:45 a.m.—halfway to their 10:30 a.m. break—they have, for all intents and purposes, eliminated the weeds. Wielding pitchforks, they begin applying mulch from a tall pile next to the garden.

Meanwhile, up the hill, the other group has moved from the Cherry Border to the beds of the several dozen lilacs that form a path pointing in the direction of the college president's house. They are, naturally, weeding. Sue Stark and volunteer Mary Lou Gessel kneel in one bed and have a philosophical discussion. "Who is to say," Mary Lou asks as she looks up from her work, "what is a weed?" Clearly, volunteer stall can come in many and creative forms.

Back at Cunningham House, a dozen ladies, dressed for the most part in T-shirts and cotton skirts (many of them lime green), are examining the plantings in The Scott Entrance Garden outside the front door. They are members of the Valley Garden Club, which, like many such groups in suburban Philadelphia, has an organizational membership to The Scott Arboretum that entitles them to periodic talks and tours. Today, Andrew Bunting, the arboretum's curator, is about to tell them about container gardening. This subject is a particular passion for Andrew, who began at The Scott Arboretum as an intern in 1986. At the time, he recalls, four containers were in the collection. Now, he estimates there are 120—many of which he describes as "cutting-edge plants—tropicals and nontraditional annuals."

The tree peony collection has been moved several times in the history of the arboretum because of the construction of new buildings. Today, they can be found on the slope below Clothier Memorial Hall. (Photo taken 1991.)
CLAIRE SAWYERS

The Valley Garden Club files into the classroom (directly under the astronomy dome); Andrew dims the lights and begins a slide show. It seems odd that the ladies are confined in a dark room on a radiant day, but they chose a lecture over a tour, and, to be sure, the slides are impressive. Andrew shows a shot of a banana plant. "The first year, it will be 2 feet high; the second, 12 feet; and after three, it will be 20 feet." The audience murmurs approvingly.

Elsewhere in Cunningham House, many other projects are under way. In her office on the second floor, Julie Jenney, the education and special events coordinator, prepares a flyer for an upcoming tree peony workshop, then draws illustrations for *Passport*, a special booklet to be distributed to kids on Arbor Day. Her assistant, Allison Necaise, is back from picking up the tree seedlings. At this point, she is 100 percent devoted to Arbor Day: the scavenger hunt, the demonstrations, the giveaways. Last year, more than 500 people attended, and the weather was horrible. The forecast this year is for bluer skies. Stacked next to her desk are a dozen or so giant tubs of peanut butter, which Allison will add to pine cones to make bird feeders for the kids. A longtime Arbor Day tradition is the giving out of shoe planters: old

In its present configuration, the tree peony collection is interplanted with bulbs, perennials, and wisterias trained as standards. (Photo taken 2000.)
HARRY KALISH

footwear stuffed with soil and seedlings. In one corner of Allison's office is a giant-sized plastic garbage bag filled with what looks like a couple of thousand dollars' worth of slightly used high-end size 12 athletic shoes. Yesterday, a Swarthmore student, a varsity runner, came in with it and donated the contents to the cause.

The magnolia collection of Asiatic cultivars creates clouds of blossoms in early spring. (Photo taken 1996.)
CLAIRE SAWYERS

In the office next door, Claire Sawyers, who has been the director of the arboretum since 1990, is juggling several tasks. A lot of them relate to what will happen down the road. This arboretum, after all, is one where planning ahead is appropriate. This morning, she is putting the final touches on the itinerary for an associates' trip to South Africa, 17 months hence, and also making plans for the arboretum's biannual plant sale, only four-and-a-half months away. The wrinkle, though, is that the traditional site of the very popular sale, the Rugby Field, will be unavailable; it will be turned into a parking lot during the renovation of the adjacent DuPont Science Building into a state-of-the-art science center, scheduled for completion in 2004. So the sale will be moved to a playing field at the other end of campus. It's a good location, with more parking and high visibility, but change, especially to long-standing tradition, always introduces unexpected variables, and Claire wants to make sure there are no surprises.

Outside, as the sun rises in the sky and the heat gathers, other undertakings proceed. The volunteers have finished their tasks for the day, but all over the campus, 14 men and women under the direction of Jeff Jabco, the horticultural coordinator, tend to Swarthmore's acres. Also patrolling the grounds is Plant Records Supervisor Rhoda Maurer, who, with Andrew Bunting's help, is mapping the collection using global-positioning system satellite-tracking technology. Rhoda goes from plant to plant, pointing at them with her high-tech devices; the information gets beamed up to satellites, which, in turn, provide extremely accurate readings of the plants' coordinates. By the time she is done, a couple of years from now, the arboretum will have a complete on-line map of every plant in the collection.

And if you look carefully, you see students who have decided to do their studying, not in the library stacks but on the cool grass, in the welcoming shade of a tree.

Andrew Bunting, having described container gardening in detail, has set off for Stephens Garden Creations, a nearby establishment, taking with him James Duell, the Scott's curatorial intern. They are in the market for some aquatic plants for the pond in back of Cunningham House—which the staff reckons is, for some reason, the most popular attraction in the arboretum. The main requirement is to find those that do well in the shade. Also on the shopping list is a supply of koi. All the fish in the pond perished over the winter, and during the course of the year, that amounts to a lot of fish. "Kids in town," Andrew had said before taking off, "end up dumping extra goldfish in the pond."

A few minutes after 1 p.m., 10 women gather outside Cunningham House and start walking west. To their right is the Dean Bond Rose Garden, where more than 650 rose plants, of some 200 different types, are just starting to form buds. Beyond the garden, appearing to lean on a venerable linden tree, is a double-take–inducing sight: a gigantic sculpture made of saplings woven together to resemble an ascending series of nests or cocoons. The work, called *Abracadabra*, was created by the artist Patrick Dougherty, who is responsible for some 125 such "twig sculptures" around the world. It was erected, with the help of many volunteers, over the course of three weeks during September 2000.

The women proceed past Parrish Hall, the center of the Swarthmore campus and home to most of its administrative offices; to their left is Magill Walk, a path, flanked by swamp white oaks, that leads down a long gentle hill to the Swarthmore commuter rail station, where you can catch a 25-minute train ride to Philadelphia. A half-dozen students sit on Swarthmore's trademark white Adirondack chairs, reading, studying, or just enjoying the day. A minute later, the women arrive at the top of the Scott Outdoor Amphitheater, a striking space carved out of the woods where terraced rows lead down to a grassy stage. Commencements at Swarthmore College have been held here since 1942. As the sound of chain saws drift up from the Crum Woods below, Carol Maurer, a certified aerobics instructor, gathers her nine charges, ranging in age from the mid-30s on up, and formally begins the weekly power walk. She warns them to check for ticks, leads them in some

The Dean Bond Rose Garden displays more than 600 roses. Over the years, it has become a Swarthmore College tradition for each senior to be pinned with a rosebud from this garden on graduation day. (Photo taken 1998.)

The Dean Bond Rose Garden at the height of summer bloom. (Photo taken ca. 1990.)
GOTTLIEB HAMPFLER

stretching, and sets off on their hike. (Usually Julie Jenney joins the walk to point out horticultural highlights, but today she is too busy with the Arbor Day preparations.)

The Crum Woods adjoin the Swarthmore campus and lead, after a drop in elevation of 165 feet, to Crum Creek. John Wister, the director of The Scott Arboretum from 1931 to 1969, once described the woods as "a gorgeous bit of wild Pennsylvania woodland with steep slopes, splendid outcroppings of rock, and many long vistas up and down the creek." Over the years, the arboretum has tried to achieve the delicate balance of keeping the

Beneath the oaks on Magill Walk lies a collection of daffodils.
ELEFTHERIOS KOSTANS

woods in as close to a state of nature as possible, while still maintaining it as a show-place for desirable native trees and plants.

As the power walkers descend toward the creek, they pass the Lang Music Building, from which the sounds of woodwinds rehearsing can be heard; the chain saws have evidently finished their tasks. On such a warm day, the shade of the woods is welcome, and even though not much besides the deciduous azaleas are in bloom, the concentration of green is lovely. Someone spots a deer; someone else, a snake. One of the walkers, Mary Lou Gessel, who had philosophized about weeds a few hours earlier, says she enjoys volunteering in the woods in the winter—pulling out invasive species, planting shrubs to stop erosion.

At the bottom of the hill, the woods open up into a meadow and then the creek. Just a quarter mile beyond it, hidden by concrete sound barriers, is Interstate 476, commonly known as the Blue Route, a key suburban artery. Despite the barriers, the highway's dull roar is the main soundtrack now. The walkers follow the creek's path, pointing out that trash has piled up because the water is so low.

At the same moment, as it happens, the Crum Woods Stewardship Committee is in the middle of a meeting in the President's Conference Room in Parrish Hall. Seated around a rectangular table are Claire Sawyers, Jeff Jabco, some Swarthmore professors and administrators, a student, and three representatives from an organization called the Natural Lands Trust. One of them is Roger Latham '83, a former biology professor at Swarthmore. The committee was formed a year earlier in response

One of the entrances to the Theresa Lang Garden of Fragrance found in the Clothier Cloisters. (Photo taken 2000.)
HARRY KALISH

The Scott Outdoor Amphi-theater persists as a masterful example of designing in harmony with nature. (Photo taken 1992.)
THE TERRY WILD STUDIO

to a paper written by Latham, which pointed out that because of several factors—the importance of the Woods as both an educational, scientific, and aesthetic resource and the threats it faces from invasive species, erosion, and possible development—the Crum needed a long-term plan. The Natural Lands Trust has been hired to put together that plan, and today's meeting is the first step in the process.

At the moment, the group is pondering Swarthmore students' perceptions or misperceptions of the Crum. In the latter category is the idea that the area is "wild," Claire Sawyers says. "The arboretum manages the whole campus, but some of it is managed as a natural area and some as a cultivated area," she says. "If you read early descriptions, 30,000 hemlocks were planted in the woods. Even that was cultivated, with the idea toward having Pennsylvania native species."

"It's an interesting psychological boundary," a professor says. "Some students see the Crum as the 'back lot' of the college. Is it possible to have a wild area that's completely surrounded?"

Roger Latham responds: "It depends what you mean by 'wild.' It can't be considered the same level of wild as a wilderness area out West. On some level, they are all gardens, but they're on a continuum. What we want for the Crum is for it to look like a wild area, to represent what was once a wild area. That takes a lot of work."

The committee agrees that the next step is to interview students to get a sense of what they think about—and want for—the Crum. Larry Schall, Swarthmore's vice president of administration, says that, from past experience, he knows the best way to gather a group of interviewees: put up notices that free pizza will be available in Parrish Parlors, buy a dozen boxes, and wait for the stampede. That course of action is duly moved, seconded, and unanimously approved.

The Natural Lands Trust has already started a comprehensive inventory of the Crum. Roger Latham reports that he has found "another rare species—American ginseng."

"Don't tell anyone where it is," says Claire Sawyers.

Very much on the committee's collective mind is the substantial amount of building and construction Swarthmore has done in recent years. One large project, scheduled to begin in earnest the day after commencement (about a month after this meeting), is the demolition of part of the DuPont Science Building and the construction of a replacement. In the process, the arboretum will lose—to its substantial regret—a number of trees.

Some, however, will be preserved. As the committee winds down its meeting, a member of Jeff Jabco's staff is maneuvering a vehicle with a sign announcing itself as "Big John Tree Transplanter" through the campus over to DuPont. Big John is a 90-inch tree spade, the biggest size. Swarthmore has rented it today to dig up three trees that would have gotten in the way of the DuPont transformation and move them to other spots on campus.

Leaving Parrish Hall, Jeff walks over to Big John as it comes to a stop near a three-flowered maple *(Acer triflorum)*, a lovely specimen, 30 feet high or so; the species once received a gold medal award from the Pennsylvania Horticultural Society.

The plan had been to do all this weeks earlier, he says. "But it's been rainy, and we had to wait till the soil was dry enough. Otherwise, the truck would get stuck."

A half-dozen students and professors have left their labs and offices to watch. As one member of the crew mans the controls and two others make sure the tree is properly wrapped and placed, four giant shovel-like pieces close in on the trunk. When they have it surrounded, they dig into the earth, effortlessly it seems, and finally lift the tree, roots and all. Big John rotates it 90 degrees, to a horizontal position, and starts back toward Trotter Hall—where, earlier, it had dug a big hole.

A view of Cosby Courtyard from Parrish Hall. (Photo taken 1998.)
HARRY KALISH

Claire Sawyers has arrived to watch the procedure; as she looks on, she is joined by Carr Everbach, a Swarthmore engineering professor who specializes in acoustics. Concerned about the noise that will be generated by the science center construction, he has been testing out his sound meter to measure Big John's din. "You should know it wasn't so bad," he tells Claire.

Big John places the maple in the hole. It fits. The crew members eyeball it and signal adjustments. When it is straight, the four blades come out of the ground, one at a time. The whole process has taken 16 minutes.

The day is winding down. The horticultural staff stops work at 4:30 p.m. It is still hot, but the angle of the light gives the plants and flowers a calm and stately look. Back at Cunningham House, Andrew Bunting and James Duell have returned empty-handed. Neither Stephens Garden Creations nor a second place they tried, J. Franklin Styer Nurseries, had any suitable water plants, so the greening of the pond will have to wait. Andrew walks up to the second floor to help Allison Necaise paint T-shirts for Arbor Day. James Duell repairs to the Wister Greenhouse, next to Cunningham House, which was state of the art when it was built, nearly 25 years ago, but is now bursting at the seams and patched with duct tape and glue. Replacing it is high on Claire's wish list; she has raised about $400,000 to do so. James has in front of him a task he must repeat every 7 to 10 days this time of year. It's peak season for aphids, whitefly and mealybugs, and he spends a couple of hours cutting back coleus, flowering maple, and salvias to expose the pests and then spraying them with an insecticidal soap.

*Crabapples (*Malus*) near Bond-Worth Hall. Today, most of the crabapple collection rings the Cunningham Fields. (Photo taken 1998.)*
HARRY KALISH

Claire Sawyers makes a couple of calls to people who had said they wanted to donate trees to the arboretum. A little past 6 p.m., she closes her windows and notices the crabapple in full and glorious bloom. Walking out, she sees Julie Jenney, who had waited for some quiet time to make some editorial changes on the next issue of the arboretum's newsletter *Hybrid*. When she leaves, Allison is still busy with cutting and pasting and photocopying for the Arbor Day handouts.

At around 9:30 p.m., Allison finally goes out the door. It's dark, and the temperature has comfortably retreated to about 70 degrees. As she walks to her car, Allison can hear the dull hum of the Blue Route in the distance.

Chapter 1

A High and Beautiful Location

Before Swarthmore College had a student body, a campus, or even a name, it had a Board of Managers. These 16 men and 16 women, meeting in 1863 to set policy for a school the Hicksite branch of the Society of Friends had been planning for years, decided it would be situated "in a rural district within convenient access to the city of Philadelphia." The proximity to the city was important because of the need to attract part-time teachers. The location was important so the beauties and rhythms of nature would alternately inspire, humble, and instruct the students. (This was in keeping with Quaker thought and practice. When George Fox, a founder of the sect, bequeathed land to the Friends Meeting in 1690, he stipulated some of it had to be used "for a Garden to plant with physical plants for Lads and Lassies to know Simples, and to learn to make Oils and Ointments.") Soon afterward, a name was chosen (in honor of England's Swarthmoor Hall, the home of Fox and his wife, Margaret), and 80 acres were purchased for $21,447. They were on undeveloped land in Delaware County, at the West Dale stop of the Philadelphia and West Chester Railroad, some 10 miles from the city, and they were beautiful. One of the college fathers had trod the tract and enthused about it as "the most beautiful country, dotted with houses and well-cultivated farms. The silvery waters of the Delaware were seen in two places in the far distances."

Most of the site was cornfields, but its western portion was a wooded natural ravine that sloped down to Crum Creek. This section was uninhabited and included at least one trail preserved from Indian times. A contemporary horticultural census taker named Ferris Price found 700 species of wildflowers in the vicinity, including orchids, gentians, laurel, arbutus, spring beauties, violets, wild azaleas, and asters.

Swarthmore College opened its doors in 1869. One of the founders, Lucretia Mott, marked the occasion by planting two red oaks (both now, alas, deceased). In his remarks, the president, Edward Parrish, concluded with a vivid and somewhat alarming horticultural metaphor: "The Society of Friends chiefly aims, by its system of training, to develop the innate genius of truth and goodness implanted by the Creator in every soul. As these are cultivated and grow, their effect is to choke out the weeds which would otherwise mar and deface the garden of the heart." At its beginning, Swarthmore had fewer than 200 students—both college and preparatory—and one large structure, then known simply as the College Building and later as Parrish Hall in honor of President Parrish. Swarthmore's prospectus described the building's impressive capacities: "Besides the necessary collecting and school rooms, it contains a Library, Museum and Chemical Laboratory, adapting it to the purposes of advanced education, and parlors, dining room, kitchen, dormitories,

A tree-planting ceremony marked the ground breaking for Parrish Hall in 1869. Lucretia Mott is standing just to the right of the tree between two men.

Photographed by Broadbent & Phillips,   1206 Chestnut Street, Philada.

INAUGURATION OF SWARTHMORE COLLEGE,
PLANTING OF THE TREES.

bathrooms, and every convenience for the comfort and health of a large number of resident pupils." The College Building occupied a commanding perch, with a boardwalk path leading down to the railroad station below. Before intervening structures arose, and the quality of the air declined, observers reported that from the top of the building, they could see William Penn's statue atop Philadelphia's City Hall.

Before President Edward Magill had oaks planted, a boardwalk led from Parrish Hall to the Swarthmore train station. (Photo taken 1869.)

As early resident Susanna Gaskill-Mahan put it, "This high and beautiful location was chosen for healthfulness and seclusion by which the first managers of the college, to provide our children with a higher education, which should be guarded from some of the extravagance and unwholesome influences (particularly intemperance), which had gradually invaded the older colleges, and to give girls an equal opportunity with boys."

The college expanded in 1874, with the purchase of an adjacent 93-acre farm that included the house in which the renowned painter Benjamin West was born. (West Dale was named after his family.) And a town began to grow up around the college. The name of the railroad station was changed from West Dale to Swarthmore, and in 1880, a land company began offering residential lots for sale. Soon Swarthmore would be incorporated as a borough with paved streets, a sewer system, a school district, and a business center (on land purchased from the college, with the stipulation that liquor would never be sold or manufactured on it).

In September 1881, an explosion in the chemistry laboratory at the top of the College Building started a fire that gutted the building; for the ensuing year, faculty and students were forced to move their instruction and themselves to the adjacent town of Media, Pa. In retrospect, the disaster seems to have hardened the resolve of the young college. The wider world took note as well. Litterateurs John Greenleaf

SWARTHMORE COLLEGE

The swamp white oaks (*Quercus bicolor*) were planted in 1881.

Whittier, Oliver Wendell Holmes, Henry Wadsworth Longfellow, and Francis Parkman sent complete sets of their works to help replenish the library. Prudently, the college raised money for a new science and engineering building, Trotter Hall. Work commenced on re-creating the College Building and proceeded with sufficient swiftness that the 1882 school year could commence in its proper location. The fire also coincided with the founding and inspired the name of Swarthmore's student newspaper, which announced in the first edition, "As our patron, *The Phoenix*, arose from her ashes more glorious than before, so shall the halls of our Alma Mater rise from her ruins more beautiful, more lasting, and more useful than ever."

From the very beginning, the college was attentive to nature. It appears that the original tract contained but two trees, and as a result, from the beginning, a great emphasis was put on procuring and nurturing more. One of the first superintendents, Thomas Foulke, affectionately referred to as "Cousin Thomas," was known for buying seedlings at his own expense and planting them around campus. In 1879, President Edward Magill had two rows of 31 swamp white oaks planted to line the path (subsequently known as Magill Walk), leading from the train station up to Parrish Hall; the idea was "to form a very fine avenue in course of time."* For years, it was customary for senior classes to mark their graduation with the planting of a

* Although the trees make an impressive canopy today, they took a long time to grow. In 1892, a student publication jokingly cautioned, "Students must not pluck leaves from the oak trees on either side of the asphaltum, for fear of injuring their growth." Three years later, when their average height was only 25 feet, the man who planted them, Josiah Hoopes, wrote: "They have been a great disappointment to me for the reason that they are the best growers of any species of oak that we have in the nursery, doing equally well on high ground as low. The original order ... was to plant the Pin Oak (*Quercus palustris*) but as we had none in the nursery, nor could we obtain any from any of the nurseries that we knew of, these were planted, as being the next best for the purpose.... These oaks are natives of low grounds, along streams, etc., where they grow vigorously, making a tree about sixty or seventy feet in height, but from some unexplained cause, the specimens at Swarthmore stood still for years.... The ground at the foot of the Swarthmore lawn near the station is a stiff clay, and when we were digging the holes I remember distinctly they would fill with water before we could get the trees planted. This may have had something to do with the poor growth our trees made in that position." In 1900, a tree expert from the U.S. Department of Agriculture concluded that June bugs were stunting the trees' growth; he prescribed a course of extermination involving trapping the pests in tubs of petroleum. Whether or not his diagnosis was correct, the trees did start to grow at a faster pace subsequently.

tree on campus. The Class of 1880 planted a red oak near Cunningham House (now the home of The Scott Arboretum), and the Class of 1881 put a purple-leaf beech nearby. Both are still standing. On October 29, 1909, the college celebrated its 40th anniversary by planting two young elm trees whose heritage stretched all the way back to the days of William Penn. In the words of a contemporary newspaper account, they were "lineal descendants of the Penn Treaty elm, in whose shade the founder of the city bargained with the Indians for right of settlement." On subsequent Founders Days, trees were planted by three governors of Pennsylvania, the governors of Delaware and Indiana, and U.S. Presidents William Howard Taft and Woodrow Wilson, who in 1913 placed a scarlet oak in the ground near the present Dean Bond Rose Garden. (The tree succumbed to construction 88 years later, in summer 2001, and was taken down.) In Wilson's address, which was marked by horticultural imagery, he called Swarthmore "a nursery of principles and honor."

Despite the plantings and the still lovely setting (now suburban rather than rural), Swarthmore College in the 1920s was something less than Edenic. As a

The rebuilt Parrish Hall in 1890.

Swarthmore College.   SWARTHMORE, Pa.

noted landscape architect and horticulturist wrote at the time, "the variety of trees is not very great, covering only about seventy species in about thirty genera, and two quite inferior trees, the Norway Maple and the Norway Spruce, are used in much larger quantities than is desirable. The planting of smaller trees, of flowering shrubs and of herbaceous plants has been haphazard.... In general, there is a surprising lack of evergreens for a college campus which is used mostly in winter, and which therefore is quite bare during most of the college year."

Crum Creek and the Crum Woods for years had been a refuge for Swarthmore undergraduates—a place for boating and swimming in summer, ice skating in winter, romantic trysts, and contemplative walks—but examining them in 1929, the same observer found they were somewhat the worse for wear. He could count only about 100 wildflowers still alive; the rest, he concluded, had been "destroyed by cutting, theft or fire." Writing a few years after his inspection, he noted the college had been "unable to give these hillsides proper care. Hence the woods were utterly neglected and were as a result in a most dilapidated condition.... There were hundreds of dead trees both standing and fallen. The undergrowth was dense and mostly of shrubs that were not particularly desirable. Poison ivy, catbriar and honeysuckle particularly were to be found in large masses, smothering other growth. The entire area constituted a most serious fire menace ... and the property was inaccessible except for a few trails and one or two rather hastily constructed paths."

The man who wrote those words was John Wister, who would be the individual most responsible for the transformation of the campus. But another man's vision made Wister's contributions possible. This was Arthur Hoyt Scott (Class of 1895), the son of E. Irvin Scott, who founded the Scott Paper Co., located in Chester, just south of Swarthmore. A. H. Scott went to work for the company after graduation and became president in 1920, but his passion was horticulture. He served as an officer of the American Peony Society and the American Iris Society; at his home in the West Oak Lane section of Philadelphia, he cultivated many notable varieties of those flowers. As early as 1915, he took an interest in beautifying the Swarthmore campus, presenting the college with 100 lilacs of different varieties to plant in a sloping lawn.* In 1920, he moved to a farm of some 100 acres in the town of Rose Valley, near Swarthmore. As Wister, a friend of Scott's, later wrote, "Here for the first time he had ample room. He at once began to plant great collections of flowering trees and shrubs like Japanese cherries, crabapples, dogwoods, lilacs, mock oranges and azaleas. He imported tree peonies from Japan and the plants today are the largest and finest to be seen in this country. His collection of peonies and iris were very large, and his Japanese iris raised from seed were probably the finest ever grown near Philadelphia. He naturalized many thousands of daffodils in his meadows where they still grow happily."

Scott did not acquire his specimens and his expertise effortlessly. It may be difficult to imagine at a time when horticultural books and magazines are ubiquitous, and every zip code boasts at least one and probably several capacious garden centers; however, in the 1910s and 1920s, gardening was a rather rarefied pursuit in the United States. One history of American horticulture, referring to this period, observes, "Most gardens, however well planned, were mere reproductions of a past age. The estate, with its expansive lawns, its woodlands and its well-designed and superbly maintained garden, was the part-time residence of only the person of wealth. These were gardens for the privileged few, cared for by professional gardeners." Scott, admittedly, was a person of wealth, but, true to the era, he was also a do-it-yourselfer, and in his efforts to improve his garden, he faced a decided lack of resources. When he wanted to see and learn about peonies, he was forced to travel to Cornell University; to study lilacs, he had to go to Highland Park in the Rochester, N.Y., area.

These experiences troubled him. Wondering if there might ever be a place near Philadelphia where homeowners would be able to see—and possibly even touch— an attractive display of the breadth of plants that could thrive in their gardens, his

---

* These didn't fare well. In 1929, an anonymous commentator—probably Scott's brother-in-law, Owen Moon—observed, "Perhaps 10% stand there this day as a 'Monument to neglect'—uncared for, untrimmed, never fertilized and never dug around, at the mercy of the lawn mower, the recipient of less care than the shade trees along the same drive."

thoughts turned to the campus of his alma mater. He found an enthusiastic audience in Samuel Palmer, head of the Botany Department at Swarthmore. In February 1925, Palmer, in turn, broached the notion, by mail, to a key figure in the tale—Robert Pyle. After graduating from Swarthmore in 1897, Pyle had briefly worked as the acting superintendent of buildings and grounds; now, he was a member of the Board of Managers of the college and head of Conard-Pyle Co., the country's most successful purveyor of mail-order roses. He was also an official of the American Association of Nurserymen; in this capacity, he was trying to lay the groundwork for two additional arboreta: a National Arboretum in the District of Columbia and one for the state of Pennsylvania. The arboretum idea simply seemed to be in the air, as Pyle indicated in his reply to Palmer's letter (using Quaker pronouns, as was his custom):

Robert Pyle, the most successful purveyor of mail-order roses in the country, was a key figure in the formation of The Scott Foundation.

I am in receipt of thine, yesterday, and am very much interested in what thee has proposed. Isn't it rather a coincident [sic] and an interesting thing, that in the same mail I should have had a letter from John C. Wistar [sic], who tells me that the Philadelphia Garden Club has just held a meeting at the home of his Mother, in which they have decided that Fairmount Park ought to have an Arboretum, and that they have appointed a committee to go after it....

An Arboretum for Swarthmore would certainly be great. Professor Sargent of the Arnold Arboretum, with whom I have been in conversation at various times, indicates that the thing to be done properly, calls for about two million dollars. I would say that in our case at Swarthmore, we could do without the second million, because we already have the location and much else that would be needed. The first million that he had in mind was for the purposes of an endowment that would adequately provide funds for the maintenance, upkeep, perpetuation of such an establishment.*

* The U.S. National Arboretum in Washington, D.C., was established by act of Congress in 1927. Nothing ever became of the plans for a Pennsylvania arboretum or one in Philadelphia's Fairmount Park, but in 1932, the University of Pennsylvania would open the Morris Arboretum in the Chestnut Hill section of Philadelphia. The Arnold Arboretum, to which Pyle referred, was and is operated by Harvard in Jamaica Plain, Mass.; its founding director was C.S. Sargent.

In spring 1926, Palmer presented to the college's Board of Managers a plan by which the entire college property would become an arboretum. The document did not tend toward moderation, stating at one point, "Should such a development take place a beautiful park-like area would arise centrally located, easy of access, surrounded by a densely populated country, of great value educationally, self-supporting, and always to the advantage and prestige of Swarthmore College." In his copy of the prospectus, Swarthmore College President Frank Aydelotte scribbled a question in the margin next to this passage: "How self-supporting[?]" But Aydelotte, who was renowned for his gift for delegating, encouraged Palmer, while making sure not to commit the college to anything. "The idea in general seems to me a wonderful one and I hope very much you can work it out," he wrote in a letter dated May 6. "I fully agree with all that you say about its possibilities, and believe that it would easily take rank along with our observatory as a feature of college work of more than local importance."*

Although Palmer spent much of 1927 visiting other arboreta for the purpose of research and comparison, nothing happened at Swarthmore. One reason was an underlying philosophical difference between Palmer and Scott: The former was primarily concerned with the study of native plants and wild species and thus not especially interested in the latter's notion of focusing on varieties—including hybrids and such non-native plants as daffodils, tulips, irises, peonies, and lilacs— that could be planted by home gardeners. Another problem was the scope of Palmer's ambitions. Following Pyle's suggestion, he had proposed a budget in the vicinity of $1 million, which, even in the booming 1920s, was a good deal more than anyone involved could foresee allocating or raising. Early in 1927, Scott wrote Palmer a pessimistic letter, doubting the Board of Managers would donate even the land needed for an arboretum and concluding, "I'm inclined to think that the best you could get would be permission to beautify the grounds." Yet another problem was Scott had become ill. In the same letter, he told Palmer his doctors had

* Aydelotte was referring to Sproul Observatory, which was completed in 1911 and housed the third most powerful telescope in the country at that time.

forbidden him to return to work for another three months, and, although he was willing to offer the arboretum project what support he could, "I am a poor reed to lean on." On Feb. 26, 1927, Scott suffered a stroke and died suddenly. He was 52.

However, his widow, Edith Wilder Scott (a member of the Swarthmore's Class of 1896); his sister, Margaret Moon; and her husband, Owen Moon (Class of 1894), did not forget his idea. In 1929, they approached President Aydelotte and offered to fund an endowment in Arthur Scott's honor; the proceeds would be used for the kind of campus plantings Scott had always wanted. Aydelotte, who had become president in 1921 and is most remembered for having started the academic Honors Program at Swarthmore, was not greatly interested in this prospect. He was about to launch a $2 million endowment campaign, the biggest such drive in the college's history. As Wister also later wrote, with a rather affectionate disdain, "Dr. Aydelotte's great hobby was golf and he knew too little about horticulture to really comprehend what Mrs. Scott had in mind." Initially, he tried to steer the discussion in the direction Arthur Scott had predicted—a mere beautification of the grounds. But Mrs. Scott would have none of it. "I regret very much that my gift has been announced for there are so many things to be discussed and decided upon," she wrote Aydelotte in May. "It must be an arboretum or I cannot … allow Arthur's name to be used in any way." She found an ally in Edward Martin, chairman of the Board of Managers and a plant devotee. At his urging, Aydelotte accepted the offer on these terms: If the endowment would pay the salary of a director and the cost of plants, the college would supply labor for the planting and subsequent care of the specimens. Mrs. Scott and the Moons agreed and put forth as director the name of John Wister.

Chapter 2

The Scott Foundation: A Vision Takes Root

Wister, who was 42 years old in 1929, had a rather remarkable background. He was a direct descendant of Caspar Wistar (subsequent generations changed the *a* in the surname to an *e*), who emigrated from Heidelberg, Germany, to Philadelphia in 1717. One of his descendants, and namesakes, was a Philadelphia physician and anatomist after whom two notable things were named: the Wistar Institute, a still-operating center of medical and scientific research, and the flower wisteria. A prominent Philadelphian of a later generation was Owen Wister, author of *The Virginian*. John Wister grew up on an estate in the then-rural Germantown section of Philadelphia, where he liked to follow around the gardener and haunt the greenhouse. At the age of 14, he grew his first study collection of flowers—some 40 different chrysanthemums. He took a degree in landscape architecture at Harvard and after graduation worked in the offices of practitioners in Philadelphia and New York. In 1917, after enlisting in the Army, he was sent to France, where he spent all his leave time visiting the great gardens of France, often sending notable specimens back to the United States.

John Wister

The recipients of some of those mailings—tree peonies, a special interest of Wister's—were Arthur and Edith Scott. Wister had met the couple about 1913. After admiring a photograph of their peony collection in a garden catalog, he made a pilgrimage to Oak Lane to see it. In an interview more than 60 years later, Wister recalled, "Mr. and Mrs. Scott gave me a bunch of flowers to take to my mother. She looked at them and nearly fell dead. They were so big. She said, 'Why, they're as big as chrysanthemums!' She had chrysanthemums in the greenhouse that grew on single stems 6 feet high. So, she said, 'We'll have to invite Mr. and Mrs. Scott over to see the chrysanthemums.' In the autumn, we invited them over,

Arthur Hoyt Scott

Edith Wilder Scott

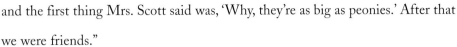

and the first thing Mrs. Scott said was, 'Why, they're as big as peonies.' After that we were friends."

Subsequently, Wister developed a national reputation as a landscape designer and a botanical expert, most notably in his work on irises. He founded and served as president of the American Iris Society and, according to one writer, "brought order out of the chaos resulting from the haphazard, indiscriminate naming of thousands of varieties. Until he had completed his studies into the origin and appearance of each plant, a name like Iris 'Purple Glory,' for instance, might have no meaning at all, either because it had been given to half a dozen different irises or because the plant so named was identical with others under different names. Mr. Wister actually unearthed one variety which had been given forty names."

Wister was in every way a logical person to direct the new Scott Foundation, but initially it was not entirely clear what that would mean. When he met with President Aydelotte about the job, Wister recalled, "He did not specify what the duties were or what he wished to have done. When I tried to pin him down a little bit more on this as to what was expected in the subsequent series of half-dozen interviews, his answer to me was always the same: 'Mr. Wister, it is always a great pleasure to me to have you come here. Please feel free to come to my office at any time, and do not hesitate to call me if I can help you.' Then he would bow me nicely out of the door without answering any of my questions."

Aydelotte did tell Wister the job would be part time, and his salary would be $1,000 a year, to be paid directly to him by Mrs. Scott.* But beyond that, the finances of The Scott Foundation were dubious at best. The endowment was widely reported in the press to be about $100,000, but that was a fanciful

---

* Even at the time, and even for a part-time position, that was not very much money. After meeting with Wister, Aydelotte wrote Mrs. Scott that there was an "expectation on both our parts that the amount of time which he gives and the salary will need to be increased as time goes on." She replied, "I am surprised he would undertake it for only $1,000 and am afraid his loyalty to us made him accept so small a sum. I know he charges far more than that for a comparatively small garden." Although the amount of time Wister spent at Swarthmore grew each year—most dramatically after 1945, when he moved from Germantown to Swarthmore—his salary did not. He continued making $1,000 a year until 1959. The following year his salary was about $500, and in subsequent years, until his retirement in 1969, he generally paid himself $100. Throughout his life, he donated all speaking fees he received to The Scott Foundation.

figure. At the end of the year, Nicholas Pittenger, Swarthmore's comptroller, tallied up the contributions at just more than $62,387. That included pledges, however. The amount of real assets collected totaled a little less than $16,000, which Pittenger reckoned would provide $1,059 in annual income—to pay for all expenditures other than the director's salary. But even that projection was optimistic. A substantial proportion of the endowment was in the form of stock. Pittenger made his accounting in December 1929. Just two months before, the market had crashed; now, as far as cash value and steady income were concerned, nothing could be less reliable than stock certificates.

CLOTHIER MEMORIAL TOWER, SWARTHMORE COLLEGE, SWARTHMORE, PA.

A postcard of Clothier Memorial Hall, which was built in 1929, the same year The Scott Arboretum was established.

On the other hand, at least for the time being, the foundation didn't really need money. There was no land or equipment to buy, no staff to pay, no offices to furnish. Wister's first task was to examine the grounds, assess the resources, and submit his recommendations. He was a superb writer (he would eventually pen four books and dozens of articles), and his three-and-a-half-page "Preliminary Report," sent to Aydelotte on Feb. 1, 1930, was cogent and readable. It was also pessimistic. Owen Moon, following his understanding of Arthur Scott's vision, had recommended putting in a series of display gardens on campus. Wister began by explaining why these would not be appropriate for the new arboretum—because of the difficulty and cost of upkeep, because "they would not present a unified appearance and might even detract from the general aspect on campus," and because there was no suitable place to put them. Instead, he advocated concentrating on the college's "greatest asset"—the Crum Woods. The portion adjoining campus, he said, "could be developed into a wild garden of great and unusual beauty unlike anything in this section of the country at a comparatively small cost." He recommended planting great quantities of rhododendrons, azaleas, mountain laurels, and other wild plants backed with dogwoods and hemlocks. This "would make a sight that would make Swarthmore famous."

Aydelotte gave his approval, and Wister began acting on the plan in the spring. Using his annual budget of barely more than $1,000, he was able to buy some 14,000 hemlocks, 10,000 rhododendrons, 5,000 dogwoods, 4,000 mountain laurel, and 400 holly. Even in 1930, this was some pretty impressive shopping. Wister was able to obtain such favorable prices by buying small. Thus, the cost of the American hemlock varied between $30 to $100 per 1,000 plants, and the plants were between 3 and 9 inches high. Too puny to face the elements, they were planted in the nursery the college maintained near Crum Creek.

Wister expected to limit his plantings to such seedlings for several years. However, as he recounted in an unpublished memoir, he was told by Edward Martin, the chairman of the Board of Managers, "that this would not do. He felt that to make the foundation known, it would be necessary to have a formal dedication of placing the first plants in a permanent and prominent location." Knowing that the lilac was Arthur Scott's favorite shrub, Wister came up with the idea of a long row of lilacs near the eastern entrance of the campus, proceeding from the meetinghouse down the lawn. Mrs. Scott gave from her garden the first two plants, both of the cultivar 'Mme. F. Morel,' which Mr. Scott had especially favored; in 1931, Wister donated 40 different others from his garden in Germantown.

Edith Wilder Scott, the widow of Arthur Scott, wields a shovel at the planting of lilacs in 1930. Despite the darkness of the day (and contrary to the Swarthmore President Frank Aydelotte's fears), the photographs of the occasion did come out.

In a letter to Owen Moon, who was not able to be present, President Aydelotte described the proceedings: "We had our first ceremony of planting the first Lilac on Tuesday in spite of the fact that it poured rain all day. Our little group of members of the Board, Faculty and student body stood on the Meeting House porch and only came out to shovel earth and be photographed. It was so dark that I am not sure the photographs will come out, but I will send you specimens of any that are successful."

The same year, Allen White, a member of the Class of 1894, and his wife gave the foundation $1,000 for the planting of Japanese cherry trees in honor of their late daughter Caroline '22. When Wister asked Aydelotte if the entire sum had to be spent on plants or whether some of it could go to manure, mushroom soil, fertilizer, and lime and other preparation, the president "replied in the usual manner, that it was a pleasure to see me and he wanted me to be sure to come in to see him next time I was there." Thus authorized, Wister was able to buy 68 cherry trees (two each of 34 varieties), about 3 to 4 feet high on average, for a grand total of $231— "leaving ample allowance for the best soil preparation I have ever seen." The trees were planted along the edge of the lawn near Cedar Lane.

The Benjamin West House depicted in an early postcard. The house, built in 1724, was the birthplace of Benjamin West in 1778 and was designated a national historic landmark in 1966. Today, it serves as a visitor center.

They were flowering by the second year, but, even so, in Wister's words, "neither the lilacs nor the cherries looked much bigger than matchsticks to the ordinary passerby." Members of the general public, unless they followed the workings of Swarthmore College very closely, would have no idea The Scott Foundation even existed. To counter that situation, Robert Pyle suggested to Wister that he plant some chrysanthemums, which would make a "quick display." Wister dug into his budget to purchase some plants, and more than 100 varieties were donated by the New York Botanical Garden and the Missouri Botanical Garden. They were placed in front of the cherry trees and were such a success the planting was repeated every autumn until World War II.

In April 1935, the *Philadelphia Record* featured a photo of a Swarthmore undergraduate, Doris Lindeman Gessner '35, in the midst of one of the cherry trees that had been planted in 1931. The caption noted, "This is the first season the trees have been in full bloom."

IT'S CHERRY BLOSSOM TIME AT SWARTHMORE

As far as the general look of the campus went, Wister's efforts were aided immeasurably by Swarthmore's head gardener, an Englishman named Harry Wood. He had been trained at the Lowther Estate in the north of England; in 1927, Robert Pyle recruited him for Swarthmore, to work under Superintendent of Grounds Andrew Simpson. Wood's arrival coincided with the first use of power machinery on campus—hitherto, the grass had been cut with hand mowers—and even before the Scott plantings took root, the grounds were looking better every year. He and Wister found they worked well together. In the words of William Frederick, who worked with them both as a Swarthmore undergraduate in the 1940s and later as a landscape designer, Wood was "a wonderful plant man. John Wister was an idea man, but Harry had the green thumb. He really knew how to make things work."

The Crum Woods, envisioned by Wister as the centerpiece of the arboretum, were in a sorry state when he arrived. As he described them, "There were quantities of dead, diseased, or broken trees. There was dreadful erosion. There were sickening piles of rubbish, old furniture, old stoves, mountains of tin cans and bottles." Clearly, many hundreds of man-hours were needed to attend to the situation. But the Swarthmore horticultural staff of a dozen or so men had already added considerable Scott-related tasks to its previous duties and could not be called on any further. Help came from an outside force—the Depression. Already, many people were losing their jobs, including workers at the Victoria Plush Mills on Crum Creek (coincidentally adjacent to the college's land), which closed in 1930. The Borough of Swarthmore raised $500 for unemployment relief, the college matched the figure, and two dozen men were put to work in the woods.

In Wister's words: "They opened trails wide enough to allow tractors and trucks to come in and haul out rubbish. They cut dead trees and firewood was sold and the proceeds added to money available to pay more workers, so that similar work could be given in the 1931 winter and for a shorter period in 1932. These men worked willingly and hard. They were not accustomed to such heavy work and suffered aching muscles and blisters at first. They were pretty clumsy compared to our own men but in the two and a half winters they literally transformed the dilapidated areas into a pleasant woodland park with attractive paths."

With that work done, Wister began to work out an ambitious plan he had for the woods. He proposed dividing it into three parts. The northern third (from Alligator Rock north to the boundary) would be confined to plant species native to Delaware County; by the middle of 1932, several thousand hemlocks and dogwoods as well as azaleas, laurels, and various ferns had already been planted. The middle section would have plants native to the entire state of Pennsylvania, and here, Wister began by putting in great numbers of *Rhododendron maximum*. The third section, bordered by the railroad tracks, would include trees and shrubs native to other parts of North America, including *R. carolinianum* and *R. catawbience*, flame azalea, silverbell, and Carolina hemlock.

Wister's scheme for the main campus was more ambitious still: to arrange plants, so far as it was possible, in a great counterclockwise circle, grouped according to their botanical family. The procession began at Wharton Hall with the ginkgo and yew and continued through the pine family to willows and poplars; through oaks and beeches to magnolias (at the library); then, to roses and the pea family; the maples; the heaths; the olive family; and, finally, in the Beardsley quadrangle, the honeysuckle family. In a note that still strikes a responsive chord with suburban homeowners, Wister observed: "Grass is one of the

The ginkgos (*Ginkgo biloba*) depicted in this postcard were removed in the 1980s because the putrid-smelling rotting fruit produced by "female" trees made residing in Wharton a trial in the fall.

WHARTON HALL,
MEN'S DORMITORY,
SWARTHMORE COLLEGE,
SWARTHMORE, PA.

most difficult plants to grow in southeastern Pennsylvania. Lawns are expensive in upkeep and are attacked by Japanese beetles and other pests, yet the Swarthmore lawns make the beauty of the campus and must be maintained. It is wise, however, to substitute under trees, where grass never does well, such plants as periwinkle, pachysandra, English ivy and native ferns."

The 1930s at The Scott Foundation were marked by a sense of possibility and excitement, as Wister—who maintained his residence in Germantown, coming down to Swarthmore a couple of times a week during the growing season, less often during the rest of the year—began to turn his vision into reality. The collection and the endowment grew, albeit modestly, and the horticultural world at large began to take notice.*

An aerial photo of the Swarthmore College campus was included as part of the 10-year history of The Scott Foundation, published in the *Swarthmore College Bulletin* in 1940.

---

* The largest single donor to the collection was Wister himself. This donation is clear from his Annual Reports, which detailed all the gifts received in the previous year. In the fiscal year 1933–1934, for example, he gave: "50 trees and shrubs in 21 species and varieties; 1,600 scions Tree Peonies in 266 varieties; 200 scions Rhododendrons in 35 varieties; 50 scions Lilacs in 11 varieties; 6 varieties Hemerocallis; 23,029 narcissus in 11 varieties; seeds of shrubs, etc." In a 10-year history of the foundation he submitted in 1939, Wister noted, with typical self-deprecation, "The Director has considered it a privilege to be able to add rare plants from his own collection from time to time. Mrs. Scott apparently requested the Director to make a charge for such plants, as there is a letter in the files stating that not only does he feel it a privilege to give the plants, but also that he would not feel that it was desirable or proper, as he is in charge of the work and of the expenditures and is receiving a regular salary, to sell any plants to the College, or to make any charge of any kind for them."

A little of the flavor of that time can be tasted from some direct quotation:

Practically all the public gardens in America have been established by botanists and built from the botanical point of view rather than from an interest in practical gardening. We have no such institution as Wisley, where horticulture comes first. It is of interest, therefore, to all gardeners to know that at Swarthmore College, near Philadelphia, Pa., a Foundation has been endowed for the encouragement of gardening by the planting of a collection of trees, shrubs, and flowers primarily of interest to the average gardener.... Philadelphia is fortunate in having a practical garden of this kind at its very door. Gardeners there will have a chance to see in a public planting, properly labeled, many of the things which they themselves could and should be growing. The planting is still young and has been growing forward slowly as the endowment has been feeling the effects of the times and funds have to be expended cautiously. Enough has been planted, however, to show how fine this planting should become in a few years.

—Lead editorial, *Horticulture*, Jan. 15, 1933

The largest individual gifts of rare plants came from the Boyce Thompson Institute in Yonkers, New York, and from Highland Park, Rochester, New York. These two gifts alone accounted for over 300 new species of trees and shrubs most of which are not in commerce and unobtainable from ordinary sources and they should be of the greatest interest to botanists for future study.

—John Wister, *Annual Report*, July 1, 1933

The most important work of the year to my mind has been one which will not be noticed by the public, namely, the beginning of carefully planned plant propagation. In August 1933 we secured through the courtesy of the Farr Nursery Company the service of a skilled propagator for several weeks. He grafted 1600 tree peonies. John Friel helped in this work and in the winter grafted a number of flowering apples, cherries and lilacs which have done exceedingly well.

—John Wister, *Annual Report*, July 1, 1934

The following plants stolen from lower nursery frames between 5 P.M., May 29, and 8 A.M., May 30:

1 Tsuga canadensis 'Compacta'

2 Taxus cuspidata 'Minima'

1 Picea excelsa 'Borealis'

1 Taxus cuspidata 'Thayeri'

2 Abies homolepsis 'Scotti'

3 Juniperus sabina 'Tamariscifolia'

These plants are from 4 to 12 inches high and were probably taken by a person with some botanical knowledge, probably a rock garden enthusiast.

We expect to offer a substantial reward, on the long chance that we may find the thief and get a conviction. We must stop the stealing of rare and valuable specimens if we are to make any progress with a scientific collection.

—Andrew Simpson, May 30, 1935

The spring bloom was quite noteworthy as many of the trees and shrubs planted in 1931 and 1932 have now become large enough to be conspicuous. The most outstanding of these were the Japanese Cherries, the flowering Crabapples, the Lilacs and the Azaleas, all of which attracted much attention.

—John Wister, *Annual Report*, July 1, 1935

Memorandum for Mr. Wood:

Somebody told me that the chrysanthemums on the east side of campus are not in very good condition, being infested with lice. I imagine you have the matter in mind, but I take the liberty of mentioning it in case you or any of the gardeners have not noticed it.

—Frank Aydelotte, Oct. 14, 1935

The march of Flowers has started on the Swarthmore campus. The first shrub to bloom was the Korean rhododendron, which demonstrated its hardiness by appearing on March 27. The forsythias were particularly fine this year, although two winters ago the buds were killed almost completely.

—Harry Wood, spring *Swarthmore College Bulletin*, April 7, 1936

Before Dutch elm disease, American elms (*Ulmus americana*) created a grand promenade in front of Parrish Hall.

The planting on the College campus as outlined in previous reports has been continued, additional trees and shrubs constantly being transferred from the nursery to their permanent places. The botanical collection is getting quite large and will soon be of importance for the study of botany.

—John Wister, *Annual Report*, July 1, 1936

In November the bank above the Chrysanthemum collection was planted to a collection of Tree Peonies, 336 plants in 132 varieties representing different color groups. These plants were all of our own propagation at Swarthmore during the summers of 1933 and 1934. This comprises what I believe to be the largest and most complete collection of Tree Peonies in the country.

—John Wister, *Annual Report*, July 1, 1937

In the late 1930s and early 1940s, Swarthmore College hosted the Pennsylvania Horticultural Society's annual Chrysanthemum Show in the Lamb-Miller Field House.

The Chrysanthemum collection flowered unusually well in the autumn and attracted much attention, bringing many visitors to the college grounds. The Pennsylvania Horticultural Society held its Chrysanthemum Show in the Girls Gymnasium on October 23rd. There were many exhibitors, and the building was well filled.... The show was so successful that The Pennsylvania Horticultural Society is planning to repeat it this year in the Field House.

—John Wister, *Annual Report*, July 1, 1938

The Daffodil collection of about one hundred varieties along the Japanese Cherry border was lifted in July, and the entire border was dug and manured. Over one hundred thousand bulbs in about 140 new varieties which had been grown for Swarthmore by Mrs. Scott and the Director were planted in the autumn.... At the present time it is estimated that the entire Daffodil plantings consist of about 150,000 bulbs.

—John Wister, *Director's Report*, July 1, 1939

Head Gardener Harry Wood contemplates a large chrysanthemum at the 1938 Show.

Chapter 3
Through Thick and Thin

For several reasons, 1940 was a milestone year. Frank Aydelotte left Swarthmore to join the Institute for Advanced Study at Princeton University. The Scott Foundation marked its 10th anniversary. And Wister completed a 657-page two-volume report titled *Swarthmore Plant Notes*. It comprised a list and detailed description of all plants growing at Swarthmore. (Wister would spend the next 15 years updating and editing the *Notes*. The 1956 edition, his last, is in the library of The Scott Arboretum Office. Typewritten and bound, it runs to more than 1,000 pages and is remarkable in its detail. For example, for just one of the Dexter rhododendrons, Wister wrote: "'Deep Pink.' with golden brown markings, 4″ diam., 5 lobes, 10 fls. Good foliage. Upright habit. Prominent scattered green-brown blotch. Stamens same color as corolla. Style pale brown-green. From Arnold Arb. 1956." Horticulturist William Frederick says of the *Swarthmore Plant Notes*: "It should be republished. It has information about cultivars of plants that you cannot get anywhere else.")

This was not Wister's only literary accomplishment in 1940. In June, he published an 89-page pamphlet that listed the accomplishments of the decade, including the planting of approximately 1,000 wild species and 4,000 horticultural varieties and looked ahead at the even greater things he planned to do in the future. But he was careful to strike a cautionary note. At this point, The Scott Foundation's endowment still totaled less than $90,000, providing an annual income of little more than $4,000. And, Wister wrote, "without greater financial resources than we have at present we cannot branch out or do much more than maintain the plants we now have." The problem was not plants—the foundation continued to receive a substantial number of gifts and, by buying small, could purchase whatever else it needed— but labor. True, the college continued to provide the services of Harry Wood and—

when things weren't too busy—the men under him. But there were now fewer of these men than there had been in 1930. Moreover, Wister argued, the foundation required more: office assistants to maintain records and communicate with the public and at least a half-dozen skilled gardeners who worked for only The Scott Foundation. All told, he estimated, the budget needed to increase to about $15,000 a year.

If this were to occur, it could be in one of two ways: the endowment could grow more than threefold, or Swarthmore College could chip in the difference. There was no sense that either would happen very soon, but 1941 was still a productive and hopeful year. The new president, John Nason, showed himself sympathetic to The Scott Foundation and its needs, and the foundation was given quarters for the first time—a small office in the basement of Beardsley Hall. Thomas McCabe '15, the chairman of the board of Scott Paper and a member of the Board of Managers,

In the original scheme for the arboretum, John Wister identified the area near the Martin Biology Building to display dogwoods. Today, this view is defined by the science center. Martin was built in 1937.
RENSHAW

donated $17,000 for the construction of a magnificent outdoor amphitheater; it was dedicated at the following year's commencement and has been the site of every commencement since 1942. The foundation gained some national recognition when Swarthmore was chosen as the site of the first annual meeting of the American Association of Botanical Gardens and Arboretums. And it achieved local visibility as a result of Wister's decision to display flowering herbaceous plants as never before. In July, a new daffodil collection, containing some 350 varieties and 15,000 bulbs, was installed in the Palmer Meadow, near Crum Creek. In the autumn, on the far side of the railroad tracks, just west of the station, Harry Wood and his minions put in a garden of 500 irises and 500 peonies. (Included in the latter were some early-flowering hybrids, which Wister described as "the largest and most complete collection of its kind in any public garden.")

Behind the tree peonies were flowering crabapple trees.

Then, Pearl Harbor was attacked, the United States entered World War II, and the grand plans of The Scott Foundation were put on hold for a long time. Far from the increase in labor Wister had hoped for, war conditions meant even fewer man-hours for the arboretum. Most notably, after Superintendent Andrew Simpson left for war work, Harry Wood took his place, leaving Wood much less time for his gardening duties. Able-bodied men were hard to come by, and, because of gasoline rationing, Wister himself could make the drive from his home in Germantown less often. As a result, he began making the difficult decision to eliminate the collections that needed the most human attention. The first to go was the display bed of chrysanthemums between College Avenue and Worth Hall. It was followed by the herbaceous plants in the president's garden and in the rock wall at the library.

But Wister did not forget his dreams, and he returned to them in 1945. It seemed a propitious time. After 16 years, he finally made the move from Germantown to Swarthmore, where he rented an apartment.* The end of the war was in sight, and in April, the foundation received the biggest publicity jolt in its history—a glowing article called "People's Garden" in America's best-read magazine, the *Saturday Evening Post*. The piece, by Arnold Nicholson, began, "There isn't a public garden anywhere in the world quite like the planting at Swarthmore College," and emphasized Arthur Scott's notion of "a floral display which the average gardener—in addition to admiring—can copy in his own back yard." Wister was presumably emboldened by the article, and as it was going to press, he drafted a 13-page memorandum for President Nason and the Board of Managers titled, "Future Plans." It outlined how, after a long period of stasis, the foundation could and should still "accomplish its original purpose." The report exuded confidence, almost a sense of manifest destiny; even the verbs and the repetitive sentence structure had a martial feel to them.

* In 1946, Wister became the first director of the John C. Tyler Arboretum, 600 acres in nearby Lima, Pa., that had been the property of the same Quaker family since 1681. It was home to the 19th-century naturalists Jacob and Minshall Painter, who in 1825 set aside some of their land to begin the systematic planting of more than 1,000 varieties of trees and shrubs. One of their descendants turned the land into a public arboretum in 1944.

Referring to the foundation, Wister wrote: "Its collections must increase in size and in importance. It must show the plants to the public in the most effective way. It should conduct demonstrations of gardening practices and publish complete reports of the various plants being grown and tested. It should conduct research in all matters pertaining to the plants in its collections, their botanical relationships, their cultivation, and their improvement by selection or plant breeding."

Carrying out the plans would require new staff, new facilities, new equipment; there, as always, was the rub. Wister estimated that the capital expenditures for the expansion he described would be between $50,000 and $150,000, and the annual cost for carrying them out would be $50,000 "or more."

Unfortunately, no amount of rhetorical confidence could turn this vision into reality. For that to have happened, John Wister would have had to be a different man. No one could have been more horticulturally knowledgeable and discerning or more dedicated to The Scott Foundation and to plants. But he was a shy man, more comfortable at the typewriter and in the garden than with people—especially large groups of people. The kind of growth he foresaw would have required, essentially, a salesman, someone willing to beat the bushes and press the flesh of potential donors and unwilling to let the door close without a check or a pledge. Wister was not that person.

Other forces were also at play. In the inflationary postwar economy, income from the college's endowment plunged. Returning veterans swelled enrollment to more than 1,000, straining college resources and placing new demands on the faculty and physical plant. Despite steep tuition increases, Swarthmore's expenditures outpaced its income in each of the fiscal years ending in 1945 to 1947. Struggling to hold the college's head above water, President John Nason launched a $5 million capital campaign in 1947. But none of the funds could be earmarked for The Scott Foundation; for many years to come, the college would have other pressing needs.

Wister would continue to direct The Scott Foundation for nearly 25 more years. Each year, the gap between his dream for the foundation and the actuality he observed grew (in his estimation) wider. In the memos and reports he furiously wrote, he no doubt overstated that gap; his total lack of interest or skill in academic politics meant that he was never able to grapple with it in an effective way. His

disappointment turned into frustration and, at times, bitterness. But his fortitude during the difficult times made it possible for the foundation eventually to experience a remarkable turnaround—the beginnings of which Wister lived long enough to witness.

In the years directly after the war, as his grand words more or less hung in the air, Wister seems to have understood the need to set his sights somewhat lower. In 1950, he wrote a two-page update to his blueprint of five years earlier; this time, his tone was sober, even grim: "I have little to add to this report. The endowment fund has not been materially increased. On account of rising costs it has become more and more difficult to maintain the present plantings."

In the years that followed, Wister adapted to a less ambitious conception of the foundation, which was not negligible. The Swarthmore campus, under his and his colleagues' care, was more and more widely recognized as one of the loveliest in the country, if not the world. For more than two decades now, students and faculty had reaped the benefits. Then, as now, most of them didn't pay much attention, but those who did were often overwhelmed by the beauty. A student in the war years, William Matchett '49, wrote a reminiscence years later that captured the spectacle of spring 1943. He recalled:

...the overpowering flood of colors and odors, of blue skies, warm days and cool evenings, azaleas, rhododendrons, daffodils on the Crum meadow, dogtooth violets in the woods, lilacs in front of the Meeting House, and cherry trees east of it....

Students gather on the steps of the Friends Meetinghouse while the blooms of weeping cherries (*Prunus subhirtella*) create curtains. (Photo taken ca. 1950.)

Beyond Wharton some of the Rhododendrons were so loaded with blossoms that their foliage was almost hidden. Wisteria cascaded from the walls of the Clothier courtyard. The daffodils ... spread across the meadow, or, even lovelier, were scattered profusely through the dark green ivy along Magill. I remember going back and putting my face into each azalea bush—wonderful autumnal russets and oranges some of them were—after I discovered that, among the odorless many, a few carried the heady fragrance of honeysuckle and cinnamon. One particular cherry tree billowed into pure white cumulus and floated above the green lawns like a moored thunderhead.

The Scott Foundation was traditionally known for its tree peonies. This one is called 'Renkaku,' or Flock of Cranes. The woman is unidentified.

Beyond the general display, some of the individual collections had developed national and international reputations. These included daffodils; irises; azaleas; magnolias; lilacs; and, certainly, tree peonies, always a special interest of Wister's. The core of the tree peony collection were donations from his own garden and that of Mr. and Mrs. Scott, supplemented with notable hybrids purchased from

Professor A.P. Saunders of Hamilton College. They were planted in a garden near Worth Hall, and, at its peak, the collection numbered some 600 specimens. In 1948, *The New York Times* termed the collection the "largest and best" in the country.

Swarthmore College   Worth Hall

A postcard from the 1950s, which is captioned: "Worth Hall is the senior women's dormitory. This is a charming group of six connected Tudor structures of gray and rust-colored stone with variegated slate roofs."

The rhododendron collection in the Crum Woods was, if anything, even more impressive. In the first five years of the foundation's existence, Wister bought some 5,000 small plants; in 1935, the Class of 1910 made a donation to purchase more than 500 larger rhododendrons and azaleas. In the years after the war, the foundation became the country's most important site for the study and propagation of Dexter rhododendrons, named after Charles Dexter, of Sandwich, Mass., who raised more than 100,000 hybrid seedlings between 1925 and 1940. For all his industry, Dexter had neglected to select, name, or introduce any of his plants into commerce. After his death, his widow began to sell the collection. In 1945, Harry Wood happened to be in Providence, R.I., and visited the Dexter nursery in Sandwich. He purchased for Swarthmore (with funds donated by Mrs. Scott) 120 plants in nine different hybrid groups—the only lot of which parentage was known—plus another 50 larger specimen plants. A few years later, a committee was formed by the American Rhododendron Society to seek out and evaluate all the Dexter hybrids, which were now located throughout the northeastern United

States. Wister was a member and wrote the eventual report; Swarthmore became the main site for testing the plants.

The first group of Dexter rhododendrons and most subsequent additions were planted near the new outdoor amphitheater and made a splendid bloom in mid-May. Unfortunately, the blossoms were all faded by early June, when the amphitheater was the site for commencement exercises. In the 1950s, the foundation conducted breeding experiments, and emerged with hybrid rhododendrons that bloomed throughout the month of June. Among the hybrids selected and named at Swarthmore are 'Tom Everett'; 'Todmorden'; 'May Moonlight'; and the late-blooming 'June Fire' and 'Lady of June,' the "most spectacular specimen in our collection and the original plant," according to Andrew Bunting.

The Scott Foundation and the Morris Arboretum of the University of Pennsylvania collaborated on an exhibit at the 1947 Philadelphia Flower Show.

In 1958, as a kind of culmination of Swarthmore's achievements with rhododendrons, Harry Wood, with the assistance of William Frederick Jr., who had graduated in 1948 and now was a landscape designer and nursery owner in Delaware, designed and installed the central attraction of the Philadelphia Flower Show—

"Rhododendron Bald." Covering more than 5,000 square feet and containing more than 1,000 plants, it represented the summit of a North Carolina mountain peak, featuring rhododendrons, azaleas, and heather. Edwin Beinecke, who underwrote the exhibit, had his gardener go to California during the winter, handpick the best specimens, and bring them back in a refrigerated truck. Among other awards, the display won the gold medal of the Flower Show.*

In 1958, the dedication of the Dean Bond Rose Garden east of Parrish Hall occurred. It had been in the works since the death of Robert Pyle seven years earlier; among his bequests was one to Swarthmore, providing for the establishment of a

Swarthmore President Courtney Smith, speaking at the dedication of the Elizabeth Powell Bond Rose Garden in 1958.

* One of the main challenges in preparing for the show was forcing the plants so they would all bloom at the same time. "We had to do some pretty fancy juggling," Frederick recalls. "We had 125 plants all together. Some were starting to bloom too fast. We put those next to a door and cracked the door open so the temperature would be next to freezing. Some buds wouldn't crack. We misted them every two hours. Finally, we put them in a furnace room. I think we were able to use all but four or five."

In the "old days," Swarthmore seniors could cut roses from the Rose Garden for their rooms. Now, that privilege is reserved for one day a year—choosing a rose to wear at commencement.

The Rose Garden as seen from a window high in Parrish Hall (ca. 1992).

rose garden in memory of Elizabeth Powell Bond [H'97], the beloved dean of women at Swarthmore from 1890 to 1906, and a great enthusiast of flowers, especially roses.* The site of the garden was the same spot where Pyle, as superintendent of grounds and buildings, had planted roses in 1898. Gertrude Smith, a garden consultant from New Jersey who had worked for the foundation each winter for several years and became assistant director in 1955, executed the design; it contained more than 900 roses of more than 200 species. (In 1964, Pyle's company, Conard-Pyle, introduced the hybrid tea rose 'Swarthmore,' in honor of the college's centennial, and a specimen was planted in the Dean Bond Rose Garden.)

Harry Wood and William Frederick '48 designed the courtyard garden for the DuPont Science Building, which opened in 1959.

* Emily Cooper, in *Dean Bond of Swarthmore, a Quaker Humanist*, wrote, "Flowers and [plant life] were a constant delight to her. In her first spring at Swarthmore, Dean Bond established a flower border from the door of her parlor to the observatory.... Through the year she decorated the dining room with flowers. Almost every autumn she had a 'chrysanthemum dinner.'" She spent the last 18 years of her life at the Germantown Friends Home and once wrote, referring to the rosebud design of her carpet, "To find myself walking upon roses that will not easily fade—what more could I ask?" After she died, in 1926, an anonymous tribute in the *Friends Intelligencer* stated, "her love for flowers and her knowledge of them was the pleasure of her life and gave her a companionship with men of learning and the tillers of the soil."

The same month as the dedication, Wood retired as superintendent of buildings and grounds, after 31 years of service. In presenting him the John W. Nason Award (for having made a distinctive contribution to the college, beyond the scope of his normal duties), Swarthmore President Courtney Smith (John Nason had resigned in 1953) said: "Harry brought with him from England the desire to create another emerald isle. The apprentice turned master has helped us to raise a meadow of daffodils, a riot of azaleas, a field house of chrysanthemums and a mountain of rhododendrons. We say of Harry Wood, 'If you require a monument look about you.'" On his retirement, Wood became a horticultural consultant for the college, and one of his first projects—again working with William Frederick—was designing and installing the garden for the new DuPont Science Building in 1959. The garden featured rocks Wood had personally spotted in the Pocono Mountains of northeastern Pennsylvania and had trucked down to Swarthmore. Wood died on Oct. 25, 1971, and in a 1973 ceremony, the garden was named the Harry Wood Garden. In the words of a memorial plaque placed among the plants, "It is a tribute to his heart, mind, and hands."

The DuPont Science Building was only one of many significant projects the college undertook in the postwar period. The expansion was problematic for the foundation, as construction of buildings and parking lots led to the diminishment or loss of several important trees or collections. Moreover, a hurricane in 1954 destroyed hundreds of trees, and a heavy snow in

In 1973, after Woods's death, the courtyard garden of the Dupont Science Building was renamed the Harry Wood Garden. William Frederick speaks at its dedication.

In 1955, the college constructed a small building for The Scott Foundation, near the Scott Outdoor Amphitheater, which held a three-dimensional map of the campus.

At the dedication, from left, are Mrs. Exton Guckes, Arthur Scott's daughter; John Wister; builder John Dornan; Edith Wilder Scott; Thomas McCabe, who funded both the amphitheater and the building; Claude Smith; Mrs. Richard Krementz, the granddaughter of Arthur Scott; and Courtney Smith, president of Swarthmore College.

1958 damaged many plants. Looking back in 1965, Wister made a melancholy tally: "We lost in this way all our Hawthorns, Mountain Ashes, Cotoneasters, Mock Oranges; most of our largest Crab Apples and Chimonanthus; most of the English Hollies ... Japanese Quince and Ghent, Knap Hill and Exbury Azaleas; three quarters of our Tree Peonies (the very worst disaster of all); the finest specimen of Cut Leaf Japanese Maple (dating back to the early 1900's); several of our best Magnolias; our only *Pinus armandi.*"

A different kind of threat reared its head in 1956. Pennsylvania's Highways Department had long envisioned a limited-access north-south road running through Delaware County, and it announced that it was choosing between two sites—a "Red" Route, which would run along the eastern border of the The Borough of Swarthmore, and a "Blue" Route, to the west, which would essentially follow the path of Crum Creek. It would also destroy The Scott Foundation's nursery, come within 200 yards of the Scott Outdoor Amphitheater (making it unusable for commencement, among other problems), and extract any remaining wilderness feel from the hills around the Crum. President Smith wrote a letter to all Swarthmore alumni, asking them to send letters of protest to Governor George Leader, and John Wister exhorted his fellow horticulturists and arboretum directors to do the same. Forty of them complied, and the American Association of Botanical Gardens and Arboretums adopted a resolution, declaring that the organization was "shocked to learn of the proposal to build an expressway through the plantings of The Scott Foundation with resultant destruction of extensive test plots and of scenic natural areas planted with outstanding collections of ornamental plants," and furthermore "that for the long term benefit of American horticulture another route for the highway should be found."*

* The Blue Route won out over the Red, but its precise location was a political football that planners, residents, politicians and various interest groups tossed around for nearly a decade. Finally, a route was chosen that was west of the original, and, as Wister noted in his 1965 annual report, "would spare most of the college property." Even so, Swarthmore College joined some Swarthmore residents to fight the Blue Route in court. That battle was finally lost in 1985, and thereupon representatives from Swarthmore College and The Scott Foundation worked closely with highway planners to ensure that the Blue Route would have the least possible environmental impact. Most notably, the southern stretch, including the part that adjoins Swarthmore, has four lanes rather than six, as originally planned; like the entire highway, it is sensitively landscaped, with high sound and sight barriers. The Blue Route, less than 22 miles long, was completed in 1992.

Wister knew that wherever the highway was placed and whatever new classroom or dorm was or was not built, this kind of "progress" was unavoidable in the second half of the 20th century. And so he began a kind of rearguard action. In 1949, Wister built a house at the southern end of campus, bordering on the Crum Woods. Shortly afterward, he later recalled, he began to plant, both in the adjacent woods and in a sunny area next to the house, "particularly rare or precious or small plants that I was afraid to plant on the main campus where they are subject to theft, vandalism, power lawn mowers in careless hands and ignorant laborers who might

John Wister autographs a copy of *The Women's Home Companion Garden Book* at a Philadelphia bookshop in 1947. To his right is Gertrude Smith, a horticulturist and, eventually, his wife.

pull them up thinking they were weeds." Wister, a lifelong bachelor, married Gertrude Smith in 1960, when he was 73 years old, and they had known each other for 26 years. (She later remarked, "It took him all that time to decide that he could take the plunge.") On joining the household, she added to the garden, with special attention to daffodils (eventually obtaining more than 400 varieties), ferns, wild flowers, rock gardens, and rock wall plants.

Wister noted: "This is a collection such as probably the main Campus can never have, but we regard it not as a private garden but as the herbaceous section of The Scott Foundation. Visitors are always welcome and indeed they are coming apparently in greater numbers than those who see the flowering shrubs and trees on the main campus. The plants are carefully labeled. We know of no similarly extensively labeled collection anywhere in this general area. We are proud of it and happy to have people come and share it with us. It has been making up in part for our disappointment of having to move Iris, Peonies and Hemerocallis over to the new Nursery and particularly of losing so many of the plants that we once hoped would become permanent parts of the Campus."

Wister continued to add to the garden until his death in 1982 (at age 95). Gertrude Wister remained in the house and cultivated the garden, with the notable assistance of a Scott staff member named James Janczewski, until her death in 1999, at age 94. The house then became faculty quarters for Swarthmore College, but the garden is still open to the public.

The Scott Outdoor Amphitheater

In the area of Crum Woods directly adjacent to Clothier Hall, there had always been a natural amphitheater. But it apparently was no longer in use by 1929, when John Wister made his initial examination of the Swarthmore grounds: His report makes no mention of it. President John Nason's *Annual Report* for 1941 notes that the amphitheater had "almost completely disappeared."

Nason made this observation because Thomas McCabe, a member of the Board of Managers and Arthur Scott's successor as head of the Scott Paper Co., had offered to pay for the construction of a new outdoor auditorium on the site. But to make the space suitable for commencement exercises and performances, numerous design challenges had to be met. The college engaged a Massachusetts landscape designer to make a preliminary study, and Wister—with the assistance of the superintendent of grounds, Andrew Simpson '19—began making plans as well. At some point, there was a disagreement over which direction to take; to resolve it, the noted Philadelphia landscape architect Thomas Sears, who had graduated from Harvard one year before Wister, was brought in to draw up the final plans. His fee was $700.

The decision did not please Edith Wilder Scott, the widow of Arthur Scott and a close friend of Wister's. She wrote to Nason: "I am so sorry John Wister and Andy Simpson were not able to have the chance for building the auditorium for all the preliminary work and planning was done by them. Of course, I may be speaking out of turn, but it seems a shabby way to treat two gentlemen who have given more than money can buy—loyalty. I feel it is a poor way and must express my disappointment and displeasure. Mr. Wister only said, '700 dollars would build quite a lovely stone wall.'"

Nason diplomatically replied: "[T]here was a certain disagreement within the Property Committee concerning the nature of the outdoor auditorium and the proper procedure to be taken. The wisest way of breaking the deadlock seemed to be to call in another person. John Wister himself was asked to get in touch with the best landscape architect in Philadelphia aside from himself, to tell him what we wanted done, and to arrange the fees with him and in general put him in charge. I wanted it to be perfectly clear that we were not going over his head.

"I agree with John that the fee which we are paying Mr. Sears would build quite a lot of stone wall, and that his plan is very close to the one which John drew up. On the other hand it is a maneuver which has satisfied everyone completely, and will make it possible to go ahead with the auditorium in complete harmony."

The project, which cost a total of $16,572.69, was completed in time for commencement exercises in 1942, which seemed to mend fences and showcase The Scott Foundation. John Wister and Edith Scott each received honorary degrees—

This fanciful outdoor theater was proposed by architect E.L. Tilton. Quaker traditions of simplicity and economy eventually held sway.

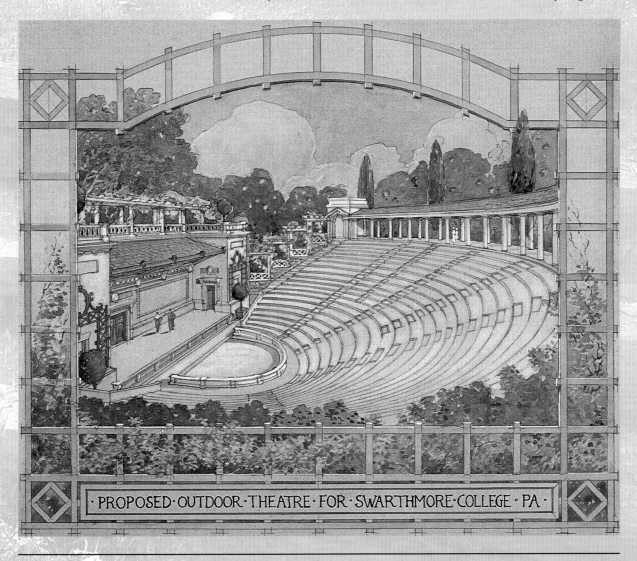

PROPOSED · OUTDOOR · THEATRE · FOR · SWARTHMORE · COLLEGE · PA ·

his a doctor of sciences, hers a master of arts. Richardson Wright, the editor of *House and Garden* magazine, received the Scott Medal, and C. Stuart Gager gave an address on "Theatres, Gardens, and Horticulture."

Swarthmore sent invitations to the exercises to representatives of dozens of arboreta, horticultural societies, and garden clubs, and the reviews were positive. Frank Waugh of Massachusetts State College wrote to Swarthmore's Robert Pyle: "I think you have one of the finest outdoor theaters at Swarthmore to be found anywhere in the [United States].... The acoustical properties of the theater are practically perfect. We were sitting far back but could hear practically every syllable uttered on stage."

In the more than 60 years of its existence, the Scott Outdoor Amphitheater, with its terraces of natural stone and grass, its high ceiling of majestic tulip poplars, has been a memorable setting for many concerts and plays (although since the completion of the Blue Route in the 1990s, the dull roar of traffic has made the

The Scott Outdoor Amphitheater in spring 1997.
CLAIRE SAWYERS

acoustics somewhat less ideal than those experienced by Frank Waugh). To Swarthmore students, however, it is known and remembered most of all as the site of commencement.

The events of 1983 proved just how important the tradition is. That year, because of heavy rain and predicted thunder squalls, commencement was moved out of the amphitheater (and into the Lamb-Miller Field House) for the first time since 1942. David Fraser, who had become president of Swarthmore the previous November, recalled the day:

The seniors were glum. Small groups pleaded to have the decision reversed. Muttering was heard up and down the ragged line of graduates as they formed along the indoor track in preparation for the 10 a.m. start of the ceremonies. Our decision was looking especially suspect because it had stopped raining. One more group of students cornered me and Professor Paul Mangelsdorf Jr. '49, marshal for the commencement exercises, asking that they be allowed to march up to and through the Scott Amphitheater so they might at least see it on graduation day. Paul and I agreed that if it could be done briskly commencement would not be much delayed.... So without warning the faculty, Board, or assembled parents (or many of the seniors), we went to the head of the seniors' line, executed a U-turn out of the field house and marched up the hill. As we reached the Sproul Observatory, I turned to Paul and alerted him that I planned to surprise the seniors by conferring degrees on them in the amphitheater. He led them down the steps to the places where they would have sat on a sunnier day and I stepped up on the platform: "By the power vested in me by the Commonwealth of Pennsylvania and the Board of Managers...."

The seniors were absolutely still. I knew my lines but was not at all certain that the Board had vested this power in me—after all, members of the Board were all down in the Field House. When I finished the seniors shouted and cheered. They had trudged up the hill to the amphitheater but they now skipped back down it. It was of more importance than a newcomer might have at first suspected that a Swarthmore tradition—in this case, of graduating outdoors—remained unbroken.

Chapter 4

The End of an Era

In autumn 1959, the president of Swarthmore College, Courtney Smith, appointed a commission to study the status of The Scott Foundation. The human impetus for the action, needless to say, was John Wister. Wister had turned age 72 that year, and as he grew older, he seemed to grow less satisfied with his and the foundation's lot. He certainly did not get any less willing to speak his mind. A year earlier, he sent Smith a three-and-a-half-page "report on problems of The Scott Foundation." The problems, as usual, came down to money and manpower, especially the latter. The most pressing need was for a full-time gardener, but in general, Wister complained, the college was simply not providing enough labor to the foundation; as a result, many collections had been diminished or even lost as a result of inadequate care. The problem was felt most dramatically in the weeks before Parents' Day and commencement. This was a critical moment in the growing season, when men were desperately needed, but year after year, he complained, the college pulled them away to spruce up the campus. He concluded with a familiar warning: "The deterioration of many of these collections is serious. If arrangements cannot be made to improve them, then they should be curtailed and where necessary given up entirely … so that those which remain can be adequately cared for."

He followed this up a year later with an even stronger memo and a more specific complaint. According to Wister, Mrs. Scott (with whom he had developed a close friendship over the years) and Owen Moon had only been willing to provide the endowment for the foundation because President Aydelotte had assured them "that if the Foundation provided the Director to make the plans and choose the plants, and if it then provided the plants, the ground force of the College would plant and maintain them." Subsequent administrations, Wister suggested, had reneged on this promise. For years, one of the most significant items in the foundation's budget had been the salary of John Friel, a wizard at plant propagation, and Wister thought that under the Aydelotte agreement his paycheck should have come out of the college's budget. As before, he said that in the absence of additional support, collections would have to be eliminated. This time, he added a threat: "If, however, too many of the present collections are eliminated or too much reduced, the foundation will deteriorate into a second class institution. In this case, the Scott family may prefer to have it given up entirely."

Parrish Hall as seen from the Dean Bond Rose Garden. Because of potential damage to the mortar, the ivy was removed from the building.

A view across Parrish lawn, as it appeared in the 1960s. The American elms were replaced with tupelo trees (*Nyssa sylvatica*) in 1983.
WALTER HOLT

It may be that Wister's saber rattling had an effect. Whatever the reason, now, for what seemed the first time in decades, the college seemed to be willing to listen to his brief. College Vice President Joseph Shane '25, who was in charge of fund-raising and public relations and was a key figure in Parrish Hall, read Wister's 1958 report and sent Smith a memo that, essentially, agreed with it. "John Wister is probably right that we do need a head gardener or someone who will give his time as superintendent of grounds," Shane wrote. "It seems to me that the plant collection of The Scott Foundation has reached a maximum for a college as small as Swarthmore and one which does not use this collection in its educational program. We should not look forward to adding other things, but let us take care of what we have."

President Smith subsequently appointed a five-member Special Committee to restudy The Arthur Hoyt Scott Horticultural Foundation. The committee met twice in December 1959, examined Wister's correspondence with administration figures for a period of 30 years, and reached what may have been an inescapable conclusion: "[I]t is unfortunate that the college has not succeeded in creating satisfactory working relationships with The Scott Foundation and that the relationship has become strained as evidenced by John Wister's letters and memoranda." To improve that relationship, the committee recommended that the director of the foundation report directly to the president and "should be accorded the same consideration as any academic department head in the College." Its concluding statement must have been music to Wister's ears: "The committee strongly urges that the college give full support to the limit of its resources to the needs of the program of the Scott Foundation." Quickly, there were tangible results: Four extra men, under the supervision of the grounds foreman, David Melrose, were assigned to the foundation. In his 1961 report, Wister remarked on an improvement in the condition of some of the collections but also cautioned that others—notably the rhododendrons, azaleas, and tree peonies—were still faring poorly.

In that same report, Wister also noted the death of Edith Wilder Scott, Class of 1896, at age 85. Mrs. Scott, who never remarried after the death of her husband in 1927, had been the principal financial provider for the foundation for more than three decades.* Wister gratefully recognized that support and said:

I do not think, however, that many people realize what a tower of strength she was to the Foundation. Many of the finest plants on the Campus came from her garden. Some of these were her own originations and introductions after years of hybridizing. Among them are the Lilacs 'Scotia' and 'Todmorden'; the Iris 'George Fox' and 'Inner Light'; the Peonies 'Chichibu,' 'Rose Valley,' 'Swarthmore,' and 'War Cloud'; and the Hemerocallis 'Todmorden.'

---

* She continued to provide after her death. In her will, she left $75,000 to The Scott Foundation, which increased the endowment to nearly $300,000. She also left $15,000 to John Wister.

Mrs. Scott was always interested in the work on the Campus. Her advice was most valuable for she had an extraordinary knowledge of plants and their care. She was one of the great amateur gardeners of her day and a tremendous influence in the Garden Club of America, the Pennsylvania Horticultural Society and other horticultural organizations of which she was an officer or a member. Her garden was an inspiration to many, and few persons ever visited her without being given flowers or plant treasures to take home. She was greatly beloved and will long be remembered and missed.

In 1964, Swarthmore College celebrated its 100th anniversary and The Scott Foundation its 35th. The anniversaries seemed to bring about a fair amount of soul-searching about the original purpose, the present state, and the future course of the foundation. John Wister turned 75 years old in March. It was, he said, "long past the usual retirement age" and, finally, "time to bring in a new director." In the meantime, true to form, he drafted a 28-page, single-spaced statement that outlined the history of the foundation up to the recent changes based on the 1959 committee's recommendation. "This was helpful," Wister wrote, "but did not solve the entire problem, for the college grounds force does not have enough men to do this at the times when the labor is most needed."

He listed some of the accomplishments and high points of the preceding three-and-a-half-decades but concluded with a poignant paragraph titled "Disappointments." Wister wrote:

The Foundation has not become a really important educational institution to encourage better gardening in the community. Its publications, schools, lectures and demonstrations have been few and far between. While it has assembled beautiful and unique plant collections it has not been able to make the best use of them for various types of needed experiments with soils, fertilizers and sprays. It has not been able to enter into long term breeding projects to produce the new plants that our experience has shown to be greatly needed not merely for our local area but for the entire middle states region. It has not been able to increase its endowment enough to sustain the work it has planned to do and should do. And finally because it has not had the money to engage a proper staff and labor force it has had to allow its plant collections to deteriorate.

Knowing that Harry Wood was experienced, knowledgeable, and not given to alarmism or hyperbole, President Smith asked him to read and comment on Wister's report. In general, Wood concurred. He thought that, if anything, the foundation's mission was more important than it had ever been, because of the hundreds of thousands of people who had migrated out of the cities since the war: "A drive through any Philadelphia suburban area in the spring, summer and fall would convince one that the occupants of these houses are really interested in plants and wish to learn more about them." He seconded Wister's long-standing contention that the income from Scott Fund, coupled with the college's contributions, in both funds and man-hours was "not adequate to maintain all the collections on the Campus."

Administrators are famous for responding to problems by appointing committees, and that is what Smith did—again. But he gave this new panel some teeth—symbolized by the fact that its chairman was Swarthmore Vice President Edward Cratsley, the college's chief money man, and that the other vice president, Joseph Shane, was a member of the committee. On Nov. 10, 1964, soon after appointing the committee, the president sat down with Wister for a conversation. Immediately after meetings, Smith habitually put on paper an impressionistic account of what had occurred. His comments on this particular talk follow:

I told him that it was time, I thought, for us to try to start over again. I said that I felt unsupported by him in efforts to work for the Scott Foundation. I said that our understanding had been that his relationship to me was that of a chairman of any other department, but that he never came to me with problems in advance or problems when they were current but then would let out a blast in his annual report. I told him that I

Above: The entrance to Clothier is at left and Wharton Hall in the distance.

Above left: The most notable change in the Bond-Worth courtyard was the ivy that covered the walls; this photo shows how it looked after construction in 1928. Most of the trees in the picture no longer exist.

Left: Parrish lawn, facing the train tracks.

Swarthmore College began in 1869, on what was formerly treeless farmland. By the time the photos on these two pages were taken, roughly 100 years later, the campus was heavily wooded.

ALL PHOTOS VERNE

Right: Beyond the conifers is the Scott Outdoor Amphitheater.
Below: Trees obscure the bottom of Clothier Memorial Hall.
Below right: Another view of Clothier Memorial Hall.

could only work for the Scott Foundation if he consulted me on its problems and advised me on what needed to be protected and what needed to be done, rather than reporting in subsequent annual reports what had not been done. I spoke too of the negative attitude that had been revealed in conversation with a prominent horticulturist in New York, who reported that he understood the administration at Swarthmore was hostile to the Foundation, and I said too that I had been told by others during the Centennial Fund campaign that money was available for the Scott Foundation but that John Wister was so very negative, had turned down plants that were offered to him, and that the Foundation had no plan. I told him furthermore that I was distressed to see him using students as an instrument, and pointed out that the things he had reported to The Phoenix *interview in* The Phoenix *for November 6, 1964, were matters that should have been reported to me—that is, that if particular trees should be saved or given a high priority he should let me know that in advance, rather than stirring up students about them. [*The Phoenix *is the student newspaper. In an interview, Wister had bemoaned the loss of some historic trees on campus and tried to stir up students in their defense: "They march for Civil Rights—I would love to see them do it for the trees too!"] I told him that there were strict understandings whenever we were planning a location of a building that John must be consulted, and that the report that I always got was that John concurred in the judgment. He said that he always said 'go ahead' because he felt tired and weary and I said that that very attitude, however, kept me from being informed of his views until his next annual report would be critical of what had been done.*

One part of John's mind understands all of this, and yet fundamentally I think he does not understand it.

I told him that I have great respect for him and great affection for him, that it troubled me to say these things, and that it troubled me not to be able to have a relationship that would make it possible for me to work constructively for the Foundation. I urged (again) that we forget the past history and try to work constructively in the future.

The 1965 committee, essentially, endorsed the findings of its predecessor. But it backed up its sentiments with more detailed and, to some extent, radical conclusions and recommendations. They can be summarized as follows:

- The primary importance of the foundation was not the beautification and upkeep of the campus grounds, but rather, in keeping with Arthur Scott's original ideas, the horticultural education of the public and the college community.

- Because it had "brought about a degree of rigidity that ha[d] limited the total program," it was no longer necessary or desirable to maintain the "botanical sequence" of planting that John Wister had put into place so long ago.

Workers unearthing a magnolia tree that had to be moved for the construction of the McCabe Library.

- The staff of the foundation had long been involved in propagating and hybridizing new varieties. Given the range of plants now available in nurseries, this was no longer a wise use of resources.

- As far as John Wister's successor was concerned, the position should be re-defined as a full-time job, and furthermore the new director should be in charge not only of the foundation but of "the total horticultural interests of the College."

- Income from The Scott Foundation's endowment was not enough to appropriately compensate such a person. As a result, $250,000 from the Centennial Fund was allocated to the foundation, bringing its endowment to nearly $600,000 by 1965.

The library shortly after its completion in 1968 and an American elm, which was protected in the construction process and still stands today.

The most dramatic result of the committee's actions and recommendations was this: They allowed John Wister to decide, finally, that it was safe to retire. His 1965 *Annual Report* had a valedictory feel to it, as he acknowledged that it was possibly his final one and (characteristically referring to himself in the third person) took a moment to "express his appreciation for the help and loyalty of the present staff and student workers."

In fact, however, Wister stayed on for nearly four more years. They were, for the most part, difficult and unhappy ones. The labor crunch was eased somewhat in 1967, when David Melrose was appointed assistant director of The Scott Foundation. But the college had a difficult time finding a new "director of the Arthur Hoyt Scott Foundation and College Horticulturist" (as the position was titled)—in part, no doubt, because Wister's frequently voiced complaints both inside and outside the college made the position seem a rather unattractive one. (In another of his memos after a meeting with John and Gertrude Wister, Courtney Smith said he told them "that I felt terribly depressed about the possibility of our finding the right person given their negativism.") In 1967 and 1968, at least six separate men who had applied for the position either declined the college's offer or removed their names from consideration before an offer was made.

It certainly didn't help matters that the job search was going on during a time of protest and tension, both nationally and locally. In January 1969, a group of students from the Swarthmore Afro-American Students Society, protesting what they saw as the college's poor record in recruiting black students, occupied the Swarthmore Admissions Office. They were still there a week later, when President Smith suffered a heart attack and died. The entire episode was a very painful one for Swarthmore, on many levels, and the scars it caused took years to heal.

Ironically, just weeks later, The Scott Foundation finally found a director. He was a young man named Joseph Oppe.   ✣

Chapter 5

New Director, New Directions

Joe Oppe, who was 37 years old, had a strong horticultural background, having left a position as the director of the Dawes Arboretum in Newark, Ohio, a facility that spans more than 1,000 acres and contains more than 2,200 trees, shrubs, and woody vines. It was, coincidentally, also founded in 1929. But he was no John Wister—and, indeed, it would have been impossible, in 1969, to find someone of Wister's stature to succeed him as head of The Scott Foundation. What was fortunate, at that point in the foundation's history, was another difference between Oppe and his predecessor: The new director understood how important it was to reach out to the public, and he was willing to do so. Education was, after all, a central part of Arthur Scott's original vision, but, for a variety of reasons, it had been neglected for a long time. From the very start, Oppe—a Rotarian who was comfortable going out and pressing the flesh—wanted to restore it. *The Phoenix*, the student newspaper at Swarthmore College, ran an article about his appointment as The Scott Foundation's "first full-time director," and the anonymous writer noted that Oppe "hopes to begin a program in horticultural education designed for the layman. Classes would be open to the public."

As Oppe says now, "By 1970, Jack Wister had built up a magnificent plant collection. It was just waiting for someone to say, 'We've got to share this with the community.' And with Wister being so famous as a truly great ornamental horticulturist, to go out and sell a public program was not really very difficult."

Certainly, the most significant event of Oppe's first few years—and the most dramatic instance of public outreach in the entire history of The Scott Foundation—was the founding of The Scott Associates in 1971. Elaine Innes, who had been Wister's secretary, gathered together a group of 21 garden enthusiasts, and over the next year, these volunteers helped out in various ways, notably conducting

Harry Wood and William Frederick designed the courtyard garden for the DuPont Science Building, which opened in 1959.

tours of the grounds for schoolchildren and others. Soon it became apparent to Oppe, to Kendall Landis '48—who had recently succeeded Joseph Shane as vice president in charge of fund-raising at the college—and to others that the foundation could accommodate a much larger, and more formally organized, group of volunteers. According to Terry Shane, Joseph Shane's wife and an avid gardener, the idea of expanding the group was broached to Edward Cratsley H'78, the vice president for finance. "Ed Cratsley said he didn't want it to be organized until at least $2,000 was on hand," Mrs. Shane recalled. "My husband wrote to 40 Swarthmore alumni, asking for a $100 contribution, and all 40 sent it in."

Clearly, a pent-up demand was being tapped. The Associates of the Scott Arboretum was established in 1972 as a full-fledged, dues-paying organization with a charge of furthering the aims of the foundation through volunteer work and financial support. Terry Shane was named chair of the group, and an impressive schedule of events and activities was inaugurated: classes; workshops; spring and fall festivals (at each one, members were given a plant "dividend"); summer programs in which young people were taught plant skills; and, beginning in the fall of 1972, a quarterly newsletter, called *Hybrid*, that included news about the foundation, its activities and collections as well as how-to articles contributed by the staff. (The first issue featured David Melrose's piece "Prune Now to Prepare for Winter.") Helping in

Dave Melrose (*right*) and John Wister at the 1977 Spring Garden Festival.

most of these activities was Loretta Hodyss, whom Oppe hired as director of horticulture and who had had substantial experience in the education departments of both the Brooklyn Botanic Garden and Longwood Gardens. Hodyss was able to effect something entirely new in the long history of The Scott Foundation—a direct connection between it and Swarthmore College students—when she established a popular noncredit course on practical horticulture. The first year it was offered, 54 students applied. Most of them had to be turned away because the greenhouse could only accommodate 20 people at a time.

Taken together, the new initiatives were a resounding success. After a mere nine months of operation, the associates amassed a membership of nearly 400 people. Within a few years, the associates were paying for all expenses of the foundation's educational programs, plus a portion of the education director's salary.

Beginning in 1974, they also subsidized a yearlong paid internship to give work experience to young people—many of them Swarthmore College graduates—interested in careers in public horticulture. The first intern was Virginia Lohr '73, who subsequently became a professor of horticulture at Washington State University. The program has continued to this day, and most interns have, like Lohr, gone on to horticultural careers. Examples include Mara Baird '79, a landscape architect who would be involved in many Scott projects in the 1990s; Tim Boland, the curator of horticultural collections at the Polly Hill Arboretum; Pam Thomas, on the horticulture staff at Garden in the Woods; and Andrew Bunting, who followed his internship with two separate stints as a Scott employee, first as plant recorder, and later as curator, a position he holds at the time of this writing.

Meanwhile, the associates' roster continued to grow—it surpassed 700 by the end of the 1970s—and new initiatives continued to be established. Two significant ones began in 1980: the first foreign trip (Judith Zuk and Jane Pepper led a tour of the great gardens of England) and the first fall plant sale (under the chairmanship of Charles Cresson, it raised $4,500). Both programs proved to be greatly and increasingly popular and are now offered in alternate years.

For many years, John Wister's annual reports lamented The Scott Foundation did not have enough manpower to care adequately for its plants. Joe Oppe took this predicament to heart and, as a result, gave a very low priority to accessioning new specimens and collections. But in 1973, he had an irresistible offer. James Frorer '15 told the college he wanted to donate his collection of about 450 mature hollies, representing more than 200 cultivars, species, and hybrids, many of them quite rare. Frorer had been inspired to start accumulating hollies some 40 years earlier, when he saw George Washington's collection at Mt. Vernon. He traveled in this country,

The Frorer Holly Collection

In 1973, James Frorer (*left*), donated his collection of about 450 hollies to The Scott Foundation. Moving the hollies from Frorer's home in Delaware took 35 days. When a photograph of the event (*below*), was printed in the *Wilmington Evening Journal*, the authorities recognized Mike Baraja, the man with the shovel, as an illegal immigrant and subsequently deported him.

the British Isles, Europe, and Asia looking for hollies; while hunting for one in New Zealand, he broke his back, an injury that prevented him from serving a term as president of the Holly Society of America.

Almost as significant as the donation of the plants was Frorer's offer to pay for their transportation from his home in Wilmington, Del., to the Swarthmore campus. The ultimate cost was $100,000 ($30,000 of which established an endowment fund for the collection's maintenance). Oppe had decided the appropriate place for the collection was a four-and-a-half-acre meadow near the Crum Creek; it had previously been the home of thousands of daffodils, traditionally plucked in the spring by Swarthmore undergraduates. It took a contractor 37 days to get all the hollies there, and to do the job, his employees used 3,000 burlap squares of various sizes, two tons of rope, 600 pounds of guy wire, 300 guy stakes, 150 cubic yards of peat humus, 150 tons of cow manure, and 35 gallons of antitranspirant. Only about

The beauty of a mature Japanese maple *(Acer palmatum* 'Dissectum'*)* can be admired on the walk to Mertz Hall.
WALTER HOLT

a dozen of the hollies did not survive the trip—a remarkable record, especially considering that, because of the contractor's prior commitments, the job had to be done in the heat of July. Today, the collection is recognized as one of the finest in the eastern United States and has been designated an official Holly Arboretum by the Holly Society of America.

By this time, the foundation had a new home. At the time of Oppe's appointment, it was housed in one cramped room in the basement of the Martin Biology Building. That did not jibe with his plan to give the Foundation a bigger public profile. "When Joe saw that, he said, 'No basement,'" said Josephine Hopkins, who came to work as Oppe's secretary shortly afterward and is still with Scott, as office manager. The college, apparently believing Oppe was entitled to a honeymoon period, acceded to his wishes and moved the foundation to a small building with a domed roof near the college's northeast entrance. The dome was there

Members of The Scott Arboretum staff in 1977 (*left to right*): Harry Foulke, Dave Melrose, Josephine Hopkins, Joe Oppe, Judy Zuk, and Martha Burdick (intern).

because the building had formerly been the student astronomical observatory. Professor of Mathematics and Astronomy Susan Cunningham, who received an honorary degree in 1888, had overseen its construction in 1886.* Two years later, at her own expense, she had a house constructed next door to the observatory. She lived there until her retirement in 1906, after which generations of Swarthmore faculty and staff—including, for a time, Joseph and Terry Shane—called it home. (Because Cunningham had paid for the construction, the college, by prior arrangement, paid her $100 annual rent until her death in 1921.)

A view of The Scott Arboretum offices in Cunningham House beneath a Yoshino cherry (*Prunus x yedoensis*). The cherry succumbed in the 1990s.
THE TERRY WILD STUDIO

The small space was divided into three offices. Judith Zuk, universally known as Judy, who had replaced Loretta Hodyss in running the educational and outreach programs, shared one of them with the curatorial intern, and remembers, most of all, being cold. "The heating system was retro-fitted," she said. "Forced air came out of the ceiling, and it never got to ground level. The first year, I had to wear fuzzy

---

* Cunningham was a remarkable figure. She was introduced to astronomy by her father when she was growing up on Nantucket but had no formal education. At Swarthmore (whose faculty she joined in 1871), she equipped the observatory with a 6-inch equatorial refracting telescope, a sidereal clock, a mean-time clock, and a chronometer. In 1908, the college provided the observatory with a photographic telescope; it was subsequently lent to an observatory in Arizona, where it was used to take the first photograph of Pluto.

Soon after Joseph Oppe's arrival as director, The Scott Foundation offices moved to Cunningham House (*above*), originally built as a residence and observatory for Susan Cunningham, a professor of astronomy. The Scott Associates paid for an entrance garden (*right*), which was completed in 1980. Note the Swarthmore Friends Meetinghouse in the background.

Founded in 1971, the Scott Associates, more than any other factor, connected the foundation to the college and local community and helped put it on a sound financial footing. In 1979, the associates celebrated the foundation's 50th anniversary. Member Nancy Forbes; John Creech, that year's recipient of the Scott Medal; Margery Baker, the president of the associates; and Joseph Oppe, foundation director (*left to right*).

Cocktails with hot and cold hors d'oeuvres

Poached Salmon with Sauce Verte

Mondavi White Wine

Sliced Tenderloin of Beef with Wine Sauce
and Mushrooms

Red Bordeaux Pontet Latour 1975

Saffron Rice   Baked Squash with Walnuts   Whole Buttered String Beans

Dinner Rolls

French Chocolate Mousse

Welcome by Mrs. Arthur Baker, Jr., President of the Scott Associates

Mr. Joseph Oppe, Director of the Scott Foundation will present
the 1979 Scott Medal recipient, Dr. John Creech

Door Prize Drawing — A fifteen day trip for two to England

Presentation of prize by Mrs. Andrew J. Forbes, Dance Chairman

Dancing to the music of the Bill Willis Orchestra

Catering provided by Norman Fair

The menu and program from the celebration of the 50th anniversary of The Scott Foundation in 1979.

boots every day of the winter." She and her colleagues let the water drip all day long during the winter, so that the pipes wouldn't freeze. In 1978, the foundation expanded into the ground floor of the Cunningham House next door—a little more spacious, a little warmer. The following year, the Scott Associates threw a ball celebrating the 50th anniversary of the foundation. The proceeds—together with contributions from the Swarthmore Class of 1929—were used to pay for a garden for the entrance to Cunningham House. It was designed by George Patton and dedicated in spring 1980.

Although the Scott Outdoor Amphitheater is seldom used in the winter months, it is a special place to visit in that season.

That same year, the foundation, which had traditionally shared a greenhouse with the Biology Department, began constructing its own, next to the Cunningham House. It was a 15-by-30-foot structure, attached to a headhouse of about the same size. Thanks, in large part, to the ingenuity of Mark Michels '80, an engineering major who made significant contributions to the design, its most notable feature was its energy efficiency. As a result of heavy insulation, double-glazed acrylic windows, southern exposure, and several passive solar devices, including columns of water that collect heat during the daylight hours and warm the house during cold nights, the structure had heating costs that were about 75 percent less than those of a comparable facility of similar design. It was named the Wister Greenhouse, in honor of both John and Gertrude Wister, both of whom, though retired, were still tending their garden—and very much involved in the doings of The Scott Foundation.

Energy efficiency was a primary goal in the design and construction of the Wister Greenhouse.

Above: The dedication of
the Wister Greenhouse
in 1981.
ARTHUR ZITO

Right: Gertrude Wister
opens the new Wister
Greenhouse.

As a result of all of the construction and all the programs, The Scott Foundation had a higher profile on campus and in the community than ever before. But many of its underlying problems remained. One was John Wister's bête noire, the shortage of manpower to take proper care of the collections. Kendall Landis remembers that some time in the late 1970s, the Burpee Company offered a donation of a large quantity of daffodil and tulip bulbs. "We turned it down, because we didn't have the budget to take care of the flowers," Landis said.

As the foundation moved into its second 50 years, it embarked on a period of scrutiny—both internally and externally. In 1981, Oppe put together a 33-page report evaluating the state of the foundation. As far as the 10 major collections went, the report concluded that four—*Paeonia*, *Prunus*, *Wisteria*, and *Rhododendron*—were, on the whole, in average or below-average shape. On an administrative level, the report pointed to some vexingly familiar problems. The foundation still did not have the authority to deploy horticulture staff and thus had

Beginning in 1980, the plant sale has been a biennial institution. At an early sale, Associates Elizabeth Friend and Lynn Kippax.

Wharton courtyard contained mostly boxwoods before it was renovated in the 1980s.
THE TERRY WILD STUDIO

to rely on the cooperation of the college's Physical Plant Department, which often was not forthcoming. As in the Wister years, there were communication difficulties on higher levels as well. Oppe reported to Edward Cratsley, the vice president for finance, and he wrote (referring to himself in the third person), "the relationship of the Director to the Vice President has never been strong. The Foundation's Director does not attend the Vice President's staff meetings and generally has contact only as the need arises…. As a result of this infrequent contact, there has seldom been good communications between the two offices. The gaps which exist due to this lack of a flow of information have led to misunderstandings and have had adverse effects on the efficiency with which the Foundation operates." Oppe recommended the organizational structure be changed, so that the director of The Scott Foundation would also be designated assistant director of physical plant/grounds and have authority over the horticulture staff and scheduling.

Oppe's summary was positive: "The Foundation's 52-year history has been one of steady progress toward the achievement of the founders' goal of developing, on the College's campus, a collection of beautiful hardy, ornamental plants." Still, he concluded, "Perhaps the most important result of the staff evaluation process is that it has reaffirmed the need for further evaluations."

Oppe with Judy Zuk, then the foundation's education director and eventually his successor as director.

He may not have realized the extent to which this recommendation would be acted on by the college administration. By autumn 1981, it had appointed a four-person outside committee, chaired by William Klein, the director of the University of Pennsylvania's Morris Arboretum, to study and evaluate The Scott Foundation. The committee's report minced no words. It found "that the Foundation, as currently constituted, lacks a clear organizational character, structure, and set of priorities," and it detected, furthermore, "a form of creeping senescence that threatens important segments of the collections."

Financially, this period was a difficult one for the college as a whole. The bear stock market, which began with the energy crisis of 1973 and continued into the 1980s, had stagnated the endowment, leading not only to deferred maintenance all over campus but to discussion of cutting staff positions. The committee, of course, focused on The Scott Foundation and reported being "alarmed by the condition of the collections. They represent a serious deferred maintenance problem, which appears to have been largely ignored or unrecognized and is cause for immediate concern."

It was not necessary to read between the lines to see that, as far as Klein and his fellow committee members were concerned, it would be difficult, if not impossible, to address these problems if Oppe remained as director. They wrote: "Many of the difficulties that now seem so intractable would be alleviated if the Directorship were held by a person with status and skills in leadership and motivation."

Even before the report was issued, Oppe understood the implications of the visiting committee's analysis. Besides, he had been director since 1970, and he had always remembered something President Courtney Smith had told him during their first interview: "I find that after about ten years, a person in this kind of position had done all there is to do." The minutes of the Scott Associates Executive Committee meeting of November 19, 1981, notes Oppe's disclosure that "the entire program is under discussion and will no doubt be reorganized. In view of all this, Joe Oppe announced that he plans to leave Swarthmore within the next six months, with great regret, but appreciation for 13 [actually 12] good years." The following March, Oppe resigned to take a position as executive director of the Transition Zone Horticultural Institute in Flagstaff, Ariz. He left The Scott Foundation poised to achieve the glory that had been just out of reach.

Chapter 6

From Foundation to Arboretum

Finding Joe Oppe's successor proved almost as difficult as finding Joe Oppe had been. After Oppe left and while the search was going on, Dave Melrose, who was near retirement age himself, served as acting director. The visiting committee had recommended that the new director of The Scott Foundation "should have faculty status, or its equivalent.... The Directorship might take one of several forms: a rotating chair, a type of visiting professorship, or a staff assignment with some teaching responsibility." This notion was fine, but, combined with the rising eminence of the foundation, it tended to attract candidates who demanded higher salaries than the college, still in a constricted financial state, was interested in paying. Some in the administration also had the perception that the faculty of the Biology Department was resistant to having a new colleague foisted on them.

In December 1982, as the search was going on, John Wister died at age 95. The headline of his obituary in *The Philadelphia Inquirer* called him "the dean of horticulture in the U.S."

Dave Melrose by the Wister Greenhouse and cold frames.

After his retirement, Wister had generally maintained good health, although with the years, he had lost mobility and needed a motorized cart to make his periodic inspections of the campus grounds and collections. He and Gertrude Wister had continued to live in their house at the edge of the Crum Woods. In March 1982, they had sent friends a "Horticultural Spring Greetings From John and Gertrude Wister" that offers a good snapshot not only of their lives but of all *kinds* of plant and animal lives as the seasons changed:

Long after their retirements, John and Gertrude Wister were vital presences around the college and the arboretum. Their garden *(right)* led from their house down to the banks of Crum Creek and changed dramatically with the seasons.

Another year, another spring. How quickly they come and go! Winter has lingered longer than usual here, and we have had two below-zero spells. But the early flowers are making a show, attracting visitors who are glad to see that spring is really here.

Birds enlivened the cold weeks. On one February day we could count twelve male cardinals flashing against the snow, and in that month we saw 29 kinds of birds from our windows. November, December and January each brought us 27 kinds. So far in March, there have been 26, but there will be more before the end of the month. Siskins quarreled over the niger seed, juncos played tag, little field sparrows came quietly to the terrace just before dusk. Only once did we see evening grosbeaks, but a towhee stayed all winter, sheltering at night in a thick holly in a southeast angle of the house. House finches and cardinals have long been singing, and now the mocking-bird and song sparrow have joined in the music.

One of us made good use of his electric cart from daffodil time until the last of the daylilies. As he always does, he enjoyed the long bloom of the lovely white Hibiscus syriacus *'Diana,' now to be found in nurseries. He has managed to reduce the daylily collection from over 600 to about 250 kinds.*

In April, daffodils bloom beneath the oaks on Magill Walk. (Photo taken 1987.)
WALTER HOLT

The rhododendrons this past spring suffered from a January mild spell which apparently caused flower buds to swell. The cold that followed killed many buds completely, and others were damaged. But the early-flowering Rhododendron, *'Strawberry Swirl,' often not very good, was never better. The mysteries of plants and gardening!*

Although we must now be stay-at-homes, we did have visits from many friends and relatives that brought us much happiness. We hope the months ahead will bring us more visits. The one of us who has just turned 95 will take you on a tour, although his cart is not big enough for two. The one of us who is about to turn 77 will walk with you, and if the sun is hot, offer you an umbrella for the walk and ice tea afterward. We'd love to see you.

The Scott Internship Program, inaugurated in 1974, has started many young people on careers in horticulture, including Andrew Bunting *(left)*, who joined the staff after his internship. In this 1986 photo, Bunting works with curatorial intern Chris Rodderick.

Above: On some days, the Theresa Lang Garden of Fragrance can offer delights for almost every sense.

Left: The Theresa Lang Garden of Fragrance. (ca. 1988).
JUDITH ZUK

Right: Curator Andrew Bunting, leading a tour in the magnolia collection in 1987.
WALTER HOLT

Below: A magical spring moment in the magnolia collection.
WALTER HOLT

Left: The Japanese scholar tree (*Sophora japonica*) grew near Trotter Hall from 1930 until 1997. A replacement tree was planted nearby in 1990 in anticipation of its loss.

Below: The Chinese Terrace in winter 1984.
BRENDAN FLYNN

Above: Magill Walk lost one of its beloved oaks in a storm in 1987. In the subsequent decade, several other of the century-old swamp white oaks (*Quercus bicolor*) have had to be replaced.
ROBERT WOOD

Right: The silver linden (*Tilia petiolaris*) planted in front of Parrish Hall pre-dated the establishment of The Scott Arboretum. Half of the tree split apart in a 1987 storm; the remainder was taken down for safety reasons in the 1990s.
ROBERT WOOD

A horticultural library was dedicated to the memory of Barbara Spaulding Cramer, a founding member of the Associates of The Scott Arboretum in 1984. Erica Glasener, education coordinator *(left)*, Linda Ransley, education intern *(center)*, and Judy Zuk *(right)* working in the library that year.

In due time, the search committee changed its objectives. Instead of eminence and a national reputation, it found someone who was young, capable, energetic—and, as a bonus, a known quantity. Judy Zuk had been the Scott's education coordinator from 1977 until 1981, when she left to pursue a Ph.D. at Cornell University. When she received a call from the search committee, she was receptive to the idea of returning to Swarthmore, she recalled, because "I was coming to the idea that I was not meant to be spending the next five years of my life looking at cells."

On her return, in summer 1983, Zuk studied the documentation relating to the founding of the foundation more than a half-century earlier. She observed (as she put it in a retrospective she wrote some years later) the institution had three principal goals: "Horticulture—to display collections of hardy plants that are the best ornamentals for gardens in the Delaware Valley; Education—to disseminate information on plants and gardening through labeling, interpretation, public programs, and publications; and Plant Evaluation—to seek out new and improved varieties to add to our plant collections, while encouraging a greater use of good garden plants." She concluded that although the second purpose was being carried out, the other two had been superseded by the more basic need to keep the collections in reasonable shape.

Director Judy Zuk, receiving a Citation of Appreciation from the American Association of Botanical Gardens and Arboreta in 1983.

But as she settled into the job, Zuk had a pleasant surprise. She found that the opportunity to devote more resources to horticulture were greater than they had been in years, thanks, in part, to the improving financial picture at the college and, in part, to the arrival of a new generation of administrators who were committed to developing The Scott Foundation as an asset. The most visible official was President David Fraser, who took office in fall 1982, succeeding Theodore Friend. But even more significant, as far as the foundation was concerned, were Director of Physical Plant Gordon Cheesman '75 and Vice President of Finance Jon Prime, to whom Zuk reported. (On the organizational flow chart, Joe Oppe had been under the director of physical plant.) "Jon was open to new ways of doing business," Zuk said. "He was willing to redirect resources. He felt that if money was needed to renew planting, money should be forthcoming." The year after her arrival, Prime authorized what Zuk calls a "huge expenditure" for the planting of more than 120 new trees and shrubs to replace the declining street trees along Chester Road.

One of Zuk's first tasks as director was removing the large trees lining Chester Road on the eastern edge of the campus and replacing them with 120 new trees.

Within Cunningham House, Zuk had an accomplished, enthusiastic, young, and comparatively large staff: Josephine Hopkins, who ran the office and, by virtue of answering the phone, was the "public voice" of the foundation; Education Coordinator Erica Glasener; Assistant Director Steve Wheaton; Jack Potter '73, who arrived shortly afterward to work in the Dean Bond Rose Garden while he was still a gardener at Wister Garden and who would become curator of the entire foundation collection; and Dave Melrose, who moved over to become director of grounds on Zuk's return but was naturally sympathetic to the foundation's needs.

As far as the collections were concerned, one important staff member was Steve Wheaton, who took over the position of director of grounds after Dave Melrose's retirement in 1984. "He was a huge ball of fire," Zuk said. "We both had the same interest in making changes. He would think nothing of digging up a 50-foot oak tree and moving it around. Steve had a great network of nursery people and plant people. He got interested in native azaleas, and would go off with a rental truck and come back with an assortment of plants for the collection that had cost almost nothing."

The purple beech (*Fagus sylvatica* 'Atropunicea') near the Cunningham House was planted as the Class of 1881 tree.

New horticultural projects, some of them of significant size, came like clockwork. In 1985, the Cherry Border was replanted and expanded, with summer flowering shrubs and perennials; the planting of a Summer Border, with 65 flowering shrubs; and the updating of the viburnums. The following year, the foundation planted late winter flowers for the witch-hazel collection.

Left: The Cherry Border—shown here soon after it was planted in 1930—was renovated in the mid-1980s.

Below: Vice President for Development Kendall Landis speaks at a ceremony celebrating the renovation of the Cherry Border.

Above: The Cherry Border ca. 1987.
WALTER HOLT

Right: Volunteer Betty Brand talks about bonsai at the 1988 Cherry Blossom Festival.

Dave Melrose *(front, right)*, superintendent of grounds, with his staff. (Photo taken 1984.)

By that time, the institution in question wasn't called The Scott Foundation anymore. After becoming director, Zuk had become increasingly convinced the name was no longer appropriate. "The word 'Foundation' implied that we gave out money," she said, "and every year, we'd get a few requests for guidelines for grant applications. I decided that 'Arboretum' would help from a marketing standpoint to clarify who we were. The important thing was retaining the name 'Scott.'" "Arboretum" was appropriate in a historic sense as well: It was the term Arthur Scott, Robert Pyle, and Samuel Palmer had used when they were first hatching the plans for the institution. Zuk wrote to some of the members of the Scott family, determined that they had no objection, and then ordered up letterhead with the new name: The Scott Arboretum of Swarthmore College.

Another, possibly even more significant, development took place around the same time. All the planting Zuk and Wheaton were doing looked lovely when it went into the ground. But it required many more person-hours for pruning, weeding, and general tending—especially considering the new emphasis on labor-intensive perennial flowers. The college administration was more amenable to the arboretum's needs, to be sure, but not to the extent of supplying all the staff these new gardens demanded. Mulling over the dilemma, Zuk and Glasener realized they had at their disposal a large, enthusiastic, mainly untapped labor pool: the Scott Associates, who by 1986 numbered some 950. And so they launched the Volunteer Training Program for Arboretum Assistants. All interested parties would get 12 training sessions, on such topics as basic botany, plant identification, and the history

Zuk and her growing staff initiated many changes during the 1980s, including changing the name of The Scott Foundation to The Scott Arboretum. Josephine Hopkins, John "Breck" Breckenridge, Zuk, Erica Glasener, and Helen Difeliciantonio (*seated, left to right*). Laurie Jeffers, Andrew Bunting, and Steve Wheaton (*standing, left to right*).

of the arboretum. In return, they would agree to help out with tours, in the greenhouse, with plant records, or getting their hands dirty in the collection. (As one former college administrator puts it, "It's a program that would make Tom Sawyer blush.") Eighteen people signed up, and their numbers have steadily increased over the years, to the current level of about 100. As much as any other factor, it is the arboretum assistants who allowed the arboretum to develop, expand, and maintain its collections so extensively from the mid-1980s to the present.

Since 1980, the Scott Associates have conducted biennial trips to see the great gardens of the world. In 1988, a group of associates flank a *Fraxinus latifola* at the Royal Botanical Gardens in Kew, England.

New steps were also taken in the second of the neglected original purposes, plant evaluation. In 1986, the arboretum became a test site for the Pennsylvania Horticultural Society's Styer Award of Garden Merit (now called the Gold Medal Award Program) and for the University of British Columbia's Plant Introduction Scheme. Two years later, it became a cooperator in the National Crabapple Evaluation Program. Several new plants were selected from the permanent collection, including *Ilex opaca* 'John Wister,' *Hamamelis mollis* 'Early Bright,' and *Itea virginica* 'Henry's Garnet,' which received the Styer Award of Garden Merit in 1988. Aided by a grant from the Institute of Museum Services, the staff invento-

A student worker preparing inventory for a plant sale in the mid-1980s.

ried, remapped, and relabeled the entire collection. And, to further the goal of encouraging the wider use of good garden plants, the biennial plant sale began, in 1985, to feature the finest plants growing at the arboretum.

Meanwhile, educational activities continued to include lectures, trips, tours, and courses and also expanded into other programs. An annual professional symposium on perennials began in 1984; by the end of the decade, it was drawing sell-out crowds of nearly 400, and was joined by other seminars. In 1987, the arboretum began to work with the Alumni Relations Office, offering an on-campus Alumni College to Swarthmore graduates for a number of years. And it regularly put together special horticultural-related exhibits in Swarthmore's McCabe Library.

To celebrate its 60th anniversary, in 1989, the arboretum constructed a new Teaching Garden behind its headquarters, including a terrace, an arbor, a small reflecting pool, and beds and borders. The garden was designed by Rodney Robinson and named for Terry Shane. That seemed appropriate, not only because she was the first chair of the Scott Associates, but because from 1951 until the late 1960s, she and her husband, Joseph, lived and gardened at Cunningham House.

At the dedication, on May 21, 1989, Mrs. Shane recalled the many people who had cultivated the site, and spoke about the wildflower garden she had put in years before: "I brought hepatica, wind-flowers, and dogtooth violets from the family farm in Bucks County; trailing arbutus and lady-slippers from our Pocono cottage; tiny red columbine from along the Hudson; bluebells from along the Brandywine; bloodroot from where the Frorer Holly Collection is now; and maidenhair fern from the Pittengers' Oxford farm. With all this churning up of the soil, I wonder if some of these same wildflowers may appear again, as happened in London after the blitzkrieg."

At the Teaching Garden dedication in 1989 (*above*), Swarthmore President David Fraser (*left*) congratulates Terry Shane.

Along Whittier Place, near the Friends Meetinghouse, an impressive sequence of American hollies (*Ilex opaca*) graces the lawn edge. (Photo taken 1989.)

HARRY KALISH

About a year later—and one year into the arboretum's seventh decade—Zuk left Swarthmore to become the president of the Brooklyn Botanic Garden. She was replaced by Claire Sawyers, a horticulturist at the Mt. Cuba Center for the Study of Piedmont Flora in Greenville, Del., and a widely published writer on horticultural subjects. She found an institution in sound shape, thanks mainly to the efforts of her predecessor. In seven years, Zuk had overseen the planting of innumerable plants, the creation of six new gardens, a doubling of the associates' membership rolls (to about 1,500), and, generally, a revival of The Scott Arboretum as a vital institution. ✺

Scott Associate President Jean Grogan and past President Lynn Kippax present a farewell gift to Judy Zuk as she departs to become president at the Brooklyn Botanic Garden in 1990.

HARRY KALISH

Chapter 7
Into a New Century

Much like the 1950s, the 1990s were an era of building and expansion on the Swarthmore College campus. The resemblance stopped, however, in one crucial respect: in this building boom, the Scott staff was consulted, and horticultural concerns were attended to, at every step of the way.

In 1990, the arboretum focused on two projects, one comparatively small and one large. The small one was on top of a new, partially underground kitchen added to Sharples Dining Hall. The rooftop was covered with tons of soil, and, because of the conditions—full sun, no irrigation system—the staff chose to make the soil sandy and to populate it with plants found naturally along seashores, including bayberry, inkberry, shore juniper, groundsel shrub, rugosa rose, and shining rose. In mid-summer, construction of the $14 million Lang Performing Arts Center was completed; in the fall, following landscape architect Rodney Robinson's design, a Winter Garden was planted surrounding the building, featuring 38 different trees and shrubs selected for their winter interest.

Volunteer Jesse Chew and curator Jack Potter putting in plants near the Lang Performing Arts Center, one of many large construction and renovation projects that transformed the Swarthmore campus in the 1990s and into the new century.

The following year, under the leadership of President Alfred H. Bloom, Swarthmore commenced planning a massive project that, in one way or another, would occupy it for the rest of the 1990s and into the 21st century: the creation of a master plan for the development of the entire campus north of Parrish Hall. Rodney Robinson was the chief landscape architect for this project as well; also involved was Mara Baird, an intern at the arboretum from 1979 to 1981. From the beginning, they and the architects responsible for designing and renovating buildings recognized the importance of coordinating both the built and the natural landscape. In an early report, the design team wrote of their interest in seeing that "architecture and landscape are joined with the express purpose of having landscape dominate the view."

Renovation work on Cunningham House in 1995.

As the North Campus Plan was refined and carried out (groundbreaking was in May 1994), landscape didn't necessarily dominate the buildings, but it was at least an equal partner. So along with the erection of a new building, Kohlberg Hall—on the site of the old Parrish Annex—came a new courtyard, funded by and named for Isabelle Bennett Cosby '28. It is a faux ruins garden that uses pillars and walls representing the foundation and supports of the former building; the plants—including trees, vines, containers, and a wide array of perennials—exhibit purple, blue, or gold foliage during the growing season.

And along with the renovation of Trotter Hall came the striking John W. Nason Garden and Outdoor Classroom, named after a former Swarthmore president and funded, in part, by a gift from the Class of 1948. The garden, defined by the four buildings that surround it—Trotter, Beardsley, Hicks, and Pearson—features plants with interesting textures year-round, especially ornamental grasses. In the late spring and early fall, its Outdoor Classroom lives up to its name, as seminars meet and ideas are exchanged amid the branches and leaves.

In 1996, a change came that Judy Zuk had long wished for—the elimination of a road on the north side of the rose garden. The remaining road became two-way, with a turnaround in the area between McCabe Library and Parrish Hall. The new flower beds in the area were filled with plants featuring (or approximating) the color garnet, in honor of Swarthmore's school color. Also arriving in 1996 was the Metasequoia Allée, between Kohlberg Hall and the Lang Performing Arts Center, featuring 18 dawn redwoods (*Metasequoia glyptostroboides*) underplanted with a tapestry of ground-covering perennials featuring white flowers and ferns.

Ground was broken in 2001 for the college's biggest project of all, a 160,000-square-foot, $77 million science center, on the site of the DuPont Science Building. Once again, walls were knocked down and old trees uprooted. (Some could be transplanted; others had to be chainsawed into firewood.) As Claire Sawyers saw it, the whole project was a temporary disruption but a long-term opportunity. Shortly after groundbreaking, she wrote:

The garden space of the Harry Wood Garden will not only be saved but expanded with the addition of a section through the renovated and expanded north side of the DuPont Science Building. In this area, we are planning to feature cultivars of Japanese maples, a popular, highly ornamental group which has been underrepresented in our collections. We will be able to better connect the cultivated campus arboretum to the trails of the Crum Woods by joining trail heads and walkways around the new building complex. We will have several new terrace areas encouraging staff, students, faculty, and visitors to step outside, relax, linger, and enjoy views of the Crum Woods and new courtyards.

Because all these projects contained significant budgets for landscaping, they gave the arboretum a chance to practice some "free" horticulture. As Sawyers put it: "We have had the opportunity to help shape the landscape without fund-raising responsibilities. The built environment, and the interface between building and landscape, give us opportunities to plant and execute our mission." More generally,

Tree spades assist with planting of the landscape around the Lang Performing Arts Center in 1990.
CLAIRE SAWYERS

in the 1990s and 2000s, a concerted effort was made to see that campus development proceeded in accordance with agreed-on long- and short-range plans. This general policy was formalized in 2002, when the joint college-arboretum Crum Woods Stewardship and Land-Use committees both issued reports setting out principles and guidelines for future building. To John Wister, this sort of responsibility and responsiveness on the part of the rest of the college would have represented an earthly paradise.

Similarly unimaginable in Wister's day was the increase in the size of the arboretum's own coffers. As a result of substantial gifts and the outstanding performance of the stock market, the value of the arboretum's various endowment funds rose from about $6 million in 1990 to nearly $20 million by 2002, from which more than $650,000 is generated annually for the arboretum and other horticultural purposes. Through the 1990s, grants and support from the associates allowed Sawyers to add two new staff positions.

While all this demolition and erection, uprooting and planting was in progress, the arboretum's educational projects continued to develop. Two successful programs were inaugurated in 1993: Arbor Day celebrations in the spring, geared to children,

The Scott Associates Celebrate 25 Years

Left: In 1996, the Associates of The Scott Arboretum celebrated the 25th anniversary of their founding.
HARRY KALISH

Below: From its original roster of 21 in 1971, the Scott Associates had grown to more than 1,000 members by the 1990s. At the associates' 25th anniversary celebration, past presidents Barbara Calkins, Jean Grogan, Lynn Kippax, Terry Shane, and Nancy Forbes (*left to right*).

Above: The celebration occurred in the Terry Shane Teaching Garden; garden hats were encouraged. Here, Peg Weaver *(center)* with her husband Quentin Weaver.
HARRY KALISH

Right: The associates noted the anniversary by giving a bronze water-feature for the Terry Shane Teaching Garden.
HARRY KALISH

that feature a variety of displays, demonstrations, and activities; and a series of three "Evenings in the Arboretum" each summer, where the public is invited to go on guided tours, followed by picnic dinners and free band or chamber music concerts in the Scott Outdoor Amphitheater.

Meanwhile, the two big programs continued alternating with each other on a biennial schedule. In even-numbered years, the associates took trips to Arizona, Scotland, Maine, England (twice), and South Africa. The plant sale got bigger and bigger, reaching a high-water mark of about $115,000 grossed in 2001. In 1999, the sale was lucky

Josephine's Gate, at the entrance to the Dean Bond Rose Garden, was installed in 1996. It was donated by Alfred Muscari, a member of the Scott Associates, in memory of his wife, Josephine, and was designed by Lydia and Greg Leavitt.

to go on at all. Two days before it was scheduled to begin, Hurricane Floyd hit the Philadelphia area, dropping a record rainfall of more than 13 inches over two days, flooding the site of the sale, Swarthmore's rugby field, and blowing down a large tent. The following day, as the staff and volunteers stood on the field discussing what to do, a large tree split and crashed down just outside the sale fence. They decided not to take that as an omen and went ahead with the sale— the field was pumped, the tent re-erected, and the plants unpacked from their boxes. The two days of the sale were sunny and mild, and the gross proceeds totaled more than $101,000.

Also, toward the end of fulfilling its educational mission (and, not coincidentally, bolstering its presence as a national institution), the arboretum with increasing frequency hosted national and regional conferences, including the annual meetings of the American Association of Botanical Gardens and Arboreta in 1998 and the Garden Writers Association of America in 2000; the Rose Society in 2002; and, every year, regional conferences devoted to woody plants and to perennials. Participants at these events invariably expressed their appreciation of the efforts of the arboretum and the state of the Swarthmore campus. As one nurseryman wrote, "The planting combinations are brilliant, and the landscaping is impeccable, but better yet, fun and adventurous…. I could go on, like about the *Sorbus alnifolia* with the little blue stems and *Salix alba* 'Chermesina' and the billowing *Amsonia hubrechtii*—but I suspect you have to go back to work. We are jaded old garden tourists and every year Swarthmore delivers a big wow—keep up the great work."

In March 1995, after a review process that took more than a year, The Scott Arboretum was accredited by the American Association of Museums: a mark of distinction achieved, at that time, by fewer than 750 of the nation's 8,500 museums. In its report, the Visiting Committee that had inspected the arboretum concluded: "The Scott Arboretum is a professionally operated institution which is accomplishing its chartered purpose very well. Its efforts and resources are prudently husbanded and are leveraged by the generous cooperation of the college itself. It achieves much more than one would expect from its rather modest income." One would have wished John Wister had lived another dozen years, if only so he could read those sentences.

His widow, Gertrude Smith Wister, *was* able to read them. After John's death in 1982, Mrs. Wister continued to be a strong presence at Swarthmore, living in their house and

Red Weaver *(left)* and Dave Melrose ready a banner to greet members of the American Association of Botanical Gardens and Arboreta, which met at The Scott Arboretum in 1998.

Above: The Entrance Garden of the Scott Arboretum offices. (Photo taken 1998.)
HARRY KALISH

Left: The Cosby Courtyard in September. (Photo taken 2000.)
DIANE MATTIS

Right: The path through the Crum Woods leading to the holly collection. (Photo taken 1998.)

Below: The Scott Arboretum offices as seen from the Terry Shane Teaching Garden. (Photo taken 1997.)

tending their garden, until summer 1999, when she died at the age of 94. She gave a bequest to the arboretum valued at about $500,000. It was 65 years after she had first become involved with The Scott Foundation and nearly 70 years after John had first come out to Swarthmore to survey the grounds and the Crum Woods.

In 1985, shortly after her 80th birthday, she received the Scott Garden and Horticultural Award. In a letter written in support of her nomination, landscape architect William Frederick '48 recalled the late 1940s, when he was a Swarthmore student:

This was a magic moment in the history of horticulture on the college campus as the beautifully meshed triumvirate of John Wister, Gertrude Smith and Harry Wood was in its prime. Each of the three had a unique point of view and a wealth of knowledge about horticulture but they worked well together because they were exuberantly enthusiastic about their work....

Gertrude Wister is among the five most knowledgeable horticulturists I have ever met. She communicates superbly both in conversation and writing about her favorite subject. She has always had time for and been most patient with young people and those less well-informed and experienced than herself. She has helped shape many careers and with her enthusiasm has 'turned the multitudes on' to gardening.

Mrs. Wister's bequest, including the value of the Wister house (the college now uses it for faculty housing), was the largest bequest in the arboretum's history. But that was only a small part of her and John Wister's legacy. The greater piece is represented by the plants themselves, so many of which received their individual attention and care. If you can find their garden—you have to turn into just the right unmarked driveway along Harvard Avenue—it's still thriving, and there for anyone to explore and enjoy. ❂

Autumn
Another Day in the Life of The Scott Arboretum

It's another unseasonably warm morning on the Swarthmore campus, this time toward the end of the year—a Wednesday in the middle of November. The sky is clear blue, as it has been for what seems forever: There's been no appreciable rainfall for at least a week, and total rain for the year is 7 inches below normal. All over campus, sprinklers are whirling and spraying, trying to give the new lawns and plants and the specimen trees a good drink before winter.

It was an odd and unsettling autumn at the arboretum, and not only because part of the campus was dug up with science center construction. The plant sale, which some associates spend two years gearing up for, was scheduled to begin on Sept. 14. When terrorists attacked on Sept. 11, 2001, preparations for the sale were already well under way. Curator Andrew Bunting brought a television set to the plant sale tent, and that evening, surrounded by exotic plants, staff and volunteers gathered around to follow the news.

Although hundreds of plants had already arrived on campus, with many more scheduled to arrive each day, and fencing, tents, and tables in place, Claire Sawyers considered canceling or postponing the sale. But the staff and the various committee heads almost unanimously thought it should go on, and so it did, in its new location on Cunningham Field across Chester Road from the main campus. There were record sales, with dozens of people coming up to Claire and other staff and volunteers to say how much they appreciated having something on which they could enthusiastically, even joyfully, concentrate their attentions on the first, difficult weekend after the attacks.

This morning, you can almost feel the air getting warmer every minute. However, the calendar cannot be denied. The first hard frost of the season came two nights ago, and the arboretum staff has been pulling up annuals, cleaning out

Above: *The John W. Nason Garden and Outdoor Classroom emphasizes texture with bold, coarse foliage contrasted to fine-textured foliage. (Photo taken 2001.)* HARRY KALISH

Right: *A view of the John W. Nason Garden and Outdoor Classroom as seen from Trotter Hall. (Photo taken 2000.)* HARRY KALISH

containers, taking in tender tubers. During the past week, they cleared out the summer display in the seasonally changing border garden in back of Cunningham House and put in pansies that could bloom all winter.

Dealing with leaves is a constant in the fall, and Horticultural Coordinator Jeff Jabco is on top of the massive job. Most leaves that fall on lawn areas are ground up by mulching lawn mowers and left on the ground to decompose. In lawn areas where the leaves are too thick for mulching, in garden beds, and on paved areas, the staff rakes the leaves, then transports them to a leaf composting area on the west side of Crum Creek. Leaves collected from residents of Swarthmore Borough and a neighboring township are brought there, too. The leaf compost is garden ready by spring, when it's available to residents to use as a soil amendment or mulch.

The Crum Creek runs through about 200 acres of woodland owned by the college and managed by the arboretum as a natural area—one of the last significant green spaces in Delaware County. (Photo taken 1990.)
THE TERRY WILD STUDIO

The mild days have made for a lot of opportunities for planting. Yesterday, two new trees were put into the Buttenwieser Terrace, and today Jeff will plant recently donated Chinese tree peonies. He'll also look at the Harry Wood Garden—which is in the sights of the bulldozers working on the new science center—and figure out which plants can be moved for replanting next week.

As the work day begins, a crew reports to the edge of the Scott Outdoor Amphitheater, where they are putting in the last of 215 native azaleas donated by Longwood Gardens, a neighboring institution about 20 miles to the west. These will be the centerpiece of a new garden commemorating the 80th birthday of Johanna Sibbett, a longtime member of the Scott Associates who is universally admired for her joie de vivre.

Gardener Sue Stark says Johanna and a friend of hers, from a Tai Chi class, were here all day yesterday, digging holes and planting azaleas.

*Tulip poplars (*Liriodendron tulipifera*) frame Parrish Hall with golden hues. (Photo taken 2000.)*
HARRY KALISH

A view of the Metasequoia Allée, facing Parrish Hall. (Photo taken 2001.)
JEFFREY HOLDER

Left center: *The swamp white oaks (*Quercus bicolor*) create an awe-inspiring canopy over Magill Walk, connecting the Swarthmore train station to Parrish Hall. (Photo taken 1991.)*
THE TERRY WILD STUDIO

Left: *A magnificent tupelo (*Nyssa sylvatica*) in Parrish West Circle creates stunning color displays. (Photo taken 1994.)*
STEVEN GOLDBLATT '67

Above: *In the fall, leaves fallen from tulip trees (Liriodendron tulipifera) transform the floor of the amphitheater from green to gold.*

Left: *Participants in a Scott Arboretum conference lunch in the amphitheater. (Photo taken 2000.)*
HARRY KALISH

In a common room at Bond Hall, on the other side of campus, 27 arboretum assistants are commencing the last of the six annual informational "updates" the arboretum offers them. This one is on tools and tool maintenance, and staffers Rhoda Maurer and Greg Paige are putting on their own version of the Home Shopping Network, topping two big tables with an array of hardware, some of it cutting-edge and some of it old-fashioned, like a pair of shrub shears. ("These are good for cutting ornamental grasses," Greg says. "But you want to think about the ergonomics.") The assistants watch and listen raptly, mentally filing away some items, no doubt, for their holiday season wish lists.

Volunteers contributed more than 500 hours to help create a temporary sculpture by Patrick Dougherty named Abracadabra *in September 2000. (Photo taken 2000.)* DIANE MATTIS

Back in Cunningham House, the staff occupies itself with various activities suitable to the season. Andrew Bunting starts compiling a list of annual vines to grow next year. Later, he teaches a volunteer, Eve Thyrum, how to imprint aluminum accession tags on the arboretum's machine. It's slow, tedious work; each letter needs to be slid into the proper place, then one must pull down on a heavy handle, like on a "one-armed bandit." Education and Special Events Coordinator Julie Jenney is thinking about next year as well, planning trips and workshops—not only the content but the instructor and (no less important!) a catchy title. After the arboretum assistant update, Rhoda Maurer goes out with Andrew to survey plants near the Friends Meetinghouse with her high-tech equipment, then processes data entry from a previous survey into the plant records database.

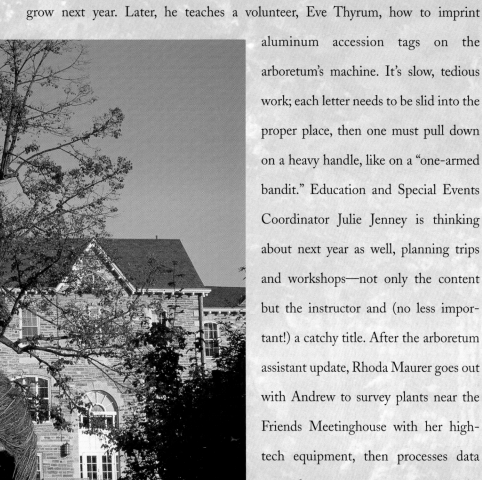

On opening the morning mail, Claire Sawyers has found an unsolicited $1,000 donation for the Greenhouse Fund, so she, at least, has one indisputably happy task among her labors today—writing a suitable thank-you note.

At 12:30 p.m., Allison Necaise greets the members of the public who have arrived for a scheduled "Weekday Highlight Tour" of the collection. There are precisely five of them, a total that includes two little girls around ages 3 and 6 and their grandparents. The autumn and winter tours typically get low attendance, which is a shame, especially on a crystalline and balmy day like today. The fall colors are blazing—the various shades of red and garnet by the Rose Garden Circle, the almost blinding yellow of the ginkgo leaves—and with most of the leaves gone, the views, once the tiny tour group gets to the Crum Woods, are extended and fine.

After the tour, back at the office, Allison helps Julie with an unexpectedly complicated task. One of the arboretum's most popular activities is a series of six wreath-making workshops planned for early December. On Julie's to-do list today

Eryngium heads backlit in the Cosby Courtyard.
ROB CARDILLO

Right: *In the Cosby Court-yard, container gardening and vines are featured. (Photo taken 2001.)*
JEFFREY HOLDER

Below: *Swarthmore College students attending language classes in Kohlberg Hall may enjoy a bird's-eye view of the Cosby Courtyard. (Photo taken 2001.)*
JEFFREY HOLDER

The Dean Bond Rose Garden with Kohlberg Hall beyond.
ROB CARDILLO

is getting hold of wreath wrap—a green tape they use to wrap sphagnum moss around a wreath frame. On top of that are stuck more greens, which, if redampened, will last for months. The problem is none of the florists or suppliers the two women call use wreath wrap—or have even heard of it—choosing instead simply to wrap the greens with wire, making for an easier process and a no less attractive product but one that will dry out in a week or so. Julie finally reaches a florist who knows what she's talking about—"Ah, the old-fashioned way," she says—but doesn't have any of the stuff in stock. Wreath wrap will live at least one more day on the to-do list.

The Scott Arboretum Offices and Terry Shane Teaching Garden. (Photos taken 2001.)
JEFFREY HOLDER

Above: *A planting referred to as the "biostream" was designed to allow storm water to recharge into the ground as it passes through this channel. (Photo taken 2000.)*
DIANE MATTIS

Above left: *Summersweet (*Clethra alnifolia*) in the foreground, with sweetly scented summer flowers, and sweet birch (*Betula lutea*) beyond, with bark that smells of wintergreen, both offer fragrances to be discovered in the Theresa Lang Garden of Fragrance. (Photo taken 2000.)*
HARRY KALISH

Left: Schizophragma hydrangeoides *'Moonlight' gracing the entrance to the Theresa Lang Garden of Fragrance.*
ROB CARDILLO

Right: *The "Evenings in the Arboretum" Program, initiated in 1993, features summer concerts of a wide variety of musical groups. (Photo taken 2001.)*
HARRY KALISH

Below: *Families picnicking in the amphitheater while attending a free concert offered as a part of the "Evenings in the Arboretum." (Photo taken 2001.)*
HARRY KALISH

Facing page: *The fall color of maples contrast with ever-greens by Clothier Tower. (Photo taken 2000.)*
HARRY KALISH

With the winter solstice barely more than a month away, the sun sets at 4:49 p.m.—more visibly than in the summer, with the leaves gone from the trees in the Crum Woods, and more majestically on a clear, still day like today. By a little after 5 p.m., it is already dark. Claire Sawyers works on writing a final report for a grant the arboretum received last year—a process she counts as only slightly less excruciating than filling out tax forms. On her way out at 5:30 p.m., she sticks her head into the workroom. She sees volunteer Eve Thyrum, who's still cranking out the metal labels, letter by letter.

A welcoming display of containers at the entrance of The Scott Arboretum offices. (Photo taken 1998.)
HARRY KALISH

The Scott Medal

When The Scott Foundation was first envisioned in the late 1920s, Arthur Hoyt Scott's sister, Margaret Scott Moon, and her husband, Owen Moon, came up with the idea of regularly presenting a gold medal and a cash award to honor persons who had made outstanding contributions to the art and science of gardening. A newspaper publisher, Owen Moon was keenly aware of the value of publicity, and he thought the Scott Medal—and the cash prize—would bring national attention to the foundation. In a pamphlet announcing the medal, Moon described its purpose as "to promote a greater love of nature, make the nation more conscious of the beauty of the outdoors, develop a greater knowledge and love of plants and flowers, spread the gospel of better planting and designing and arouse a wider interest in better planting and more beautiful gardens among all citizens."

Moon commissioned a young sculptor named Walker Hancock to design the medal, commenting to Swarthmore President Frank Aydelotte, "Mr. Hancock, I am informed, is one of the coming men in his line and will likely have a big reputation in the years to come." (This proved correct: At his death in 1998, Hancock was probably the most notable monumental sculptor in the country. His pieces include a statue of General Douglas MacArthur at the U.S. Military Academy and a bust of President George H. W. Bush in the Rotunda of the U.S. Capitol Building.)

Although the logical recipient of the first award, for 1930, would have been Liberty Hyde Bailey, the eminent American botanist and horticulturist, Moon believed the maximum publicity value could be gained from presenting it to the foundation's director, John Wister. Aydelotte demurred, writing Moon: "I am a good deal troubled by your suggestion that we should award the medal the first time to Dr. Wister. I may be wrong, but my experience would lead me to expect that for the

College to establish an award and make it first to a man on its own payroll would have the effect of preventing the rest of the country from taking it seriously." Although subsequently, an eight-member committee of distinguished horticultural experts determined the prize, Moon claimed the authority of the purse strings for the first year, and Wister was indeed the initial recipient. Bailey would have to wait until 1931.

By that time, the Depression was in full force, and Moon's stocks were no longer paying dividends. In 1932, the Scott Medal went on hiatus. It returned in 1939, and for the next 30 years was awarded, at Swarthmore College's commencement, approximately every other year.

When Joseph Oppe became director of The Scott Foundation in 1969, he quickly came to two conclusions about the Scott Medal. First, he thought it had been disproportionately awarded to people from the eastern United States, and that the scope of the selection committee should be broadened to, in his words, "represent the breadth of horticultural activity." Second, he wanted to begin awarding the medal annually. The following list makes it obvious that the second goal was accomplished. Increasing the geographical diversity of the recipients has apparently proved more difficult.

By the turn of the 21st century, the cash prize of the Scott Medal was up to $2,000 (though the medal itself has not been cast in gold since 1970). In 2003, $7,500 was given to the recipient, with an additional $2,500 given to a not-for-profit horticultural organization of the recipient's designation. Owen Moon (who died in 1947) would have been pleased to observe that the Scott Medal had become one of the two most prestigious horticultural awards in the country, along with the American Horticultural Society's Liberty Hyde Bailey Award. The recipient in the year 2000 was a westerner, Panayoti Kelaidis, Curator of Plant Collections at Denver Botanic Garden. After accepting the medal, he said, "I've been waiting for the moment, the words and, of course, there will never be a way to properly thank you for what will surely be the most gratifying and overwhelming acknowledgment of my career."

Scott Medal Winners

1930—John Wister, director of The Arthur Hoyt Scott Horticultural Foundation, Swarthmore College.

1930: John Wister *(right)* with Swarthmore College President Courtney Smith.

1931—Liberty Hyde Bailey. Bailey, born in 1858, was universally considered the most eminent figure in American horticulture. He had been the dean of the College of Agriculture at Cornell University and was editor of the *Standard Cyclopedia of Horticulture.*

1947: A.P. Saunders with his hybrid peony 'White Innocence.'

1939—J. Horace McFarland, a breeder of roses at his estate in Harrisburg, Pa., and the president of the American Rose Society. He was also the person most directly responsible for the conservation of Niagara Falls.

1941—C. Stuart Gager, director of the Brooklyn Botanic Garden and author of *Heredity and Evolution in Plants* and many other books.

1952: National Council of State Garden Clubs representatives, including Anne Wood *(second from left)* and Helen Hull *(fifth from left)* with John Wister *(center).*

1942—Richardson Wright, editor of *House and Garden* magazine and chairman of the board of the Horticultural Society of New York. From his acceptance speech: "In his time and place, Arthur Hoyt Scott was a unique figure. A successful business man, he found his greatest satisfaction in the practice of gardening—intelligent, inspired, muscular gardening. To England and the Continent, this kind of gardener—the business man gardener—is commonplace. Our American civilization has not yet reached the point where a captain of commerce naturally and simply turns to the soil and the creation of living beauty from it, as an essential part of a full life. All too many of our business men fail to realize the part they can play in the living, fluent grace of the progressing seasons. Perhaps it is just as well for most of them that the frontiers of their spirit stretch no farther than to the mediocrity of golf."

1963: Henry Skinner.

1967: Frederic Heutte.
WALTER HOLT

1944—H. Harold Hume, provost of the College of Agriculture at the University of Florida and author of the first American book on hollies. Previously, Hume had been president of the Glen Saint Mary Nurseries Company, which specialized in the development of orange and grapefruit trees, palms, and cycads.

1970: Aubrey Hildreth.

1947—A.P. Saunders, of Clinton, N.Y., who was known as America's first major hybridizer of peonies.

1949—Ellen Eddy Shaw, who, before her retirement from the Brooklyn Botanic Garden in 1945, taught the fundamentals of plant life to a quarter of a million New York City children.

1971: Donald Wyman.

1952—The National Council of State Garden Clubs. At the time, there were about 7,800 clubs nationally, with nearly 300,000 members.

1953—Benjamin Y. Morrison, a distinguished plant breeder (especially of Glen Dale azaleas and daffodils), the first director of the National Arboretum, and a long-time official with the U.S. Department of Agriculture, where, for many years, he was head of the Bureau of Foreign Plant and Seed Introduction.

1972: May Watts.
WALTER HOLT

1956—E.L.D. Seymour, editor of *The Garden Encyclopedia*.

1957—Arno Nehrling, secretary of the Massachusetts Horticultural Society.

1961—Clarence Godshalk, retired director of the Morton Arboretum near Chicago.

1973: George Lawrence *(center)* with Joseph N. Oppe *(left)* and Edward Cratsley, Swarthmore College president *(right)*.

1963—Henry T. Skinner. As director of the U.S. National Arboretum, Skinner supervised the creation of the widely used "Plant Hardiness Zone Map."

1965—Richard Farnham.

1967—Frederic Heutte, founder and retired director of the Norfolk Botanical Garden.

1974: George Avery.

1970—Aubrey Hildreth. From 1930 to 1959, Hildreth was director of the Cheyenne (Wyoming) Horticultural Field Station and was nationally known in developing plants that would thrive in high, dry climates. He moved on to become director of the Denver Botanic Gardens, retiring in 1965.

1975: Russell Seibert.

1971—Donald Wyman, horticulturist emeritus at the Arnold Arboretum and author of standard references on shrubs, trees, and vines.

1972—May Theilgaard Watts, Naturalist Emeritus of the Morton Arboretum in Lisle, Ill. From a letter supporting her nomination: "As a naturalist she has been instrumental in the preservation of a portion of the country's western prairie area. As an author and artist her books and articles have inspired untold numbers of grateful readers. Her educational projects at the Morton Arboretum and elsewhere have brought to light an appreciation of nature's intricate interaction long before the recent popular movement in ecology. No doubt her insights as a teacher have enriched and will continue to enrich and to alter generations to come."

1976: Raymond Allen *(left)* with Swarthmore College President Theodore Friend.

1973—George H.M. Lawrence. Lawrence founded the Hunt Botanical Library at Carnegie-Mellon University in 1954 and served as its director. Before that, he was Professor of Botany at Cornell.

1977: Ernesta Ballard *(left)* with Theodore Friend in the Harry Wood Courtyard Garden.

1974—George Avery, former director of the Brooklyn Botanic Garden. Avery founded *Plants & Gardens*, the popular handbook series, and remained its editor until his retirement.

1978: H. Lincoln and Laura Louise Foster with Theodore Friend.

1979: John Creech *(left)* with Margie Baker *(right)*, president of the Scott Associates.

1975—Russell Seibert, the director of Longwood Gardens in Kennett Square, Pa., and a botanist-geneticist for the U.S. Agriculture Department, serving in Haiti, Peru, and Costa Rica. From his acceptance address: "Many of us have discovered that working with plants is so pleasant because they don't talk back to us."

1976—Raymond Allen, director emeritus of Kingwood Center and past president of the American Rose Society.

1980: Clarence Lewis *(left)* with Theodore Friend.

1977—Ernesta Ballard. In 1963, she became the first woman to head the Pennsylvania Horticultural Society and in this position took the Philadelphia Flower Show to national prominence. She later became commissioner of Philadelphia's Fairmount Park.

1978—Lincoln and Laura Louise Foster, active leaders in the Rock Garden Society and writers, editors, and hybridizers. Laura Foster was known for her botanical illustrations.

1981: Elizabeth Scholtz.

1979—John Creech, director of the National Arboretum.

1980—Clarence Lewis, professor emeritus of horticulture at the State University of New York at Farmingdale and Michigan State University. From a statement by Michael Dirr, director of the University of Georgia Botanical Garden: "He has positively influenced students, nurserymen, landscape architects and the public toward the appreciation and use of superior landscape plants, and his influence on the gardening consciousness of the country is inestimable. He is a gentleman, a scholar, and a friend of horticulture."

1982: Richard Lighty.

1981—Elizabeth Scholtz, former director of the Brooklyn Botanic Garden. An expert in dye plants, she was the first woman director of a major urban botanic garden in the United States.

1982—Richard Lighty. Lighty was director of the Mt. Cuba Center for the Study of Piedmont Flora and established the research programs of Longwood Gardens in 1960. His particular interests have been in the garden use of native plants and their conservation in the wild.

1984: Thomas Everett *(left)* with Judy Zuk, The Scott Arboretum director, and Scott Associates Lynn Kippax and Herman Fritz.

1984—Thomas Everett, director of horticulture at the New York Botanical Garden and author of *The New York Botanical Garden Illustrated Encyclopedia of Horticulture.*

1985: Gertrude Wister with Swarthmore College President David Fraser.

1985—Gertrude Wister, former assistant director of both the Scott Horticultural Foundation and the Tyler Arboretum, designer of Swarthmore's Dean Bond Rose Garden, and the widow of John Wister. In support of her nomination, Richard Lighty wrote: "Gertrude is a plantperson's plantperson: one to whom experienced gardeners and professionals turn when they want straightforward answers to their more difficult plant questions. Not only has she thought deeply about gardens and garden plants, but she has grown most of what can be grown in the Swarthmore area. She is surely a master of the art and science of gardening."

1986: Fred Galle with John and Gertrude Wister.

1986—Fred Galle, horticulturist and author of *Azaleas* and other books. Galle was the first director of horticulture at Callaway Gardens in Pine Mountain, Ga.

1987: William Flemer III *(right)* with David Fraser.
PHOTOGRAPHY CENTER

1987—William Flemer III, president of Princeton Nurseries in New Jersey. Known for plant breeding and selection of shade trees, Flemer introduced such improved cultivars as 'Greenspire' littleleaf linden, 'Green Vase' zelkova, 'October Glory' red maple, 'Green Mountain' sugar maple, and 'Shademaster' honey locust.

1989: Francis Ching *(right)*
with David Fraser.
HARRY KALISH

1990: Polly Hill *(right)* with Judy Zuk.
HARRY KALISH

1991: J.C. Raulston.
HARRY KALISH

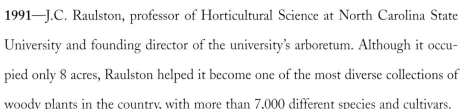

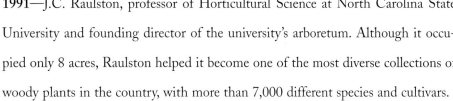

1992: Charles Lewis *(left)* with
The Scott Arboretum Director
Claire Sawyers.
HARRY KALISH

1993: Michael Dirr, professor
of horticulture at the
University of Georgia.
HARRY KALISH

1988—J. Franklin Styer. Styer was born in nearby Concordville, Pa., in 1900. After college, he worked in the family mushroom and nursery business and in 1924 became sole proprietor of J. Franklin Styer Nurseries. The Pennsylvania Horticultural Society's annual award for outstanding garden plants was named after Styer (although it is now called the Gold Medal Award).

1989—Francis Ching, director of the Los Angeles State and County Arboretum.

1990—Polly Hill, a grower, selector, and promoter of superior garden plants, whose work had led to the introduction of more than 60 new ornamentals, including the Gumpo selections of rhododendrons, which she originated from Japanese seedlings. Her collection is now the Polly Hill Arboretum on Martha's Vineyard.

1991—J.C. Raulston, professor of Horticultural Science at North Carolina State University and founding director of the university's arboretum. Although it occupied only 8 acres, Raulston helped it become one of the most diverse collections of woody plants in the country, with more than 7,000 different species and cultivars.

1992—Charles Lewis, research fellow at the Morton Arboretum in Carlisle, Ill., and an expert on the relationship between plants and people. From his acceptance speech: "Plants act as a safety valve, allowing us to relax that part of our brain that has become fatigued from having to screen portions of the environment. Glancing at plants in the office, sitting under a tree at lunch, walking under the shade of street trees will do it; will help to ease the stress of everyday life that builds within us. They are green oases where we can be refreshed."

1993—Michael Dirr, professor of horticulture at the University of Georgia and author of the standard reference source *Manual of Woody Landscape Plants*. From his remarks on acceptance: "As always, the campus is a magnificent tapestry of plants, architecture and people. Your campus has a soul; not all do."

1994—William Barrick, director of gardens at the Ida Cason Callaway Foundation in Pine Mountain, Ga., and past president of the American Association of Botanical Gardens and Arboreta. From his acceptance address: "Collectively, we must become advocates for the preservation of our gardens, natural and scenic areas, plant biodiversity, horticultural germ plasms and the environment in which we live. We must assume an active role in the horticultural and environmental education in our nation, state and world. We must align ourselves with institutions having similar goals to accomplish a broad environmental agenda. Lastly, we must all work to champion gardens as contributing significantly to the social, physical and psychological well-being of all human beings."

1995—The Pennsylvania Horticultural Society, in recognition of outreach programs like the City Gardens Contest, the largest community garden program in the country, and of the long-standing achievement of the internationally known Philadelphia Flower Show.

1996—Edward Hasselkus, professor emeritus of horticulture at the University of Wisconsin and director of the Longenecker Horticulture Gardens there.

1997—Francis Cabot, founder and director of the Garden Conservancy, an organization devoted to promoting the creation, preservation, and visitation of American gardens. With his wife, Anne Perkins Cabot, he created Stonecrop Gardens in Cold Spring, N.Y., which became a public garden in 1991.

1999: Peter del Tredici.

2000: Panayoti Kelaidis.
HARRY KALISH

2001: Marco Polo Stufano.
HARRY KALISH

2002: Harrison Flint.
HARRY KALISH

1998—Judith Zuk, president of the Brooklyn Botanic Garden and, from 1982 to 1990, the director of The Scott Arboretum.

1999—Peter del Tredici, director of living collections at the Arnold Arboretum, editor of *Arnoldia* and senior lecturer at the Harvard University Graduate School of Design.

2000—Panayoti Kelaidis, curator of plant collections at Denver Botanic Garden and an internationally recognized expert in rock gardening.

2001—Marco Polo Stufano. In 1967, Stufano was named the first director of horticulture at Wave Hill in the Bronx, N.Y. During 35 years, he led the development of Wave Hill from a deteriorating estate into one of the country's premier horticultural attractions.

2002—Harrison Flint, professor emeritus of horticulture and landscape architecture at Purdue University, who established a program for undergraduates to study public horticulture and author of several books, including *Landscape Plants for Eastern North America*.

2003—Daniel J. Hinkley, director of collections at Heronswood Nursery, on the Kitsap Peninsula in Washington State; author of several books, including *The Explorer's Garden—Rare and Unusual Perennials*.

Index

Note: Italic page numbers indicate captions for photographs.

About the Author

Ben Yagoda is a professor of English at the University of Delaware. He is the author of *About Town: The New Yorker and the World It Made* and *Will Rogers: A Biography* and the co-editor of *The Art of Fact: A Historical Anthology of Literary Journalism.* He lives in Swarthmore, Pa., with his wife, Gigi Simeone, and their two daughters.

Ben Yagoda *(right)* at the 2001 Scott Associates Plant Sale, getting guidance from plant expert George Petropoulos.
GENE SCHNIERLE

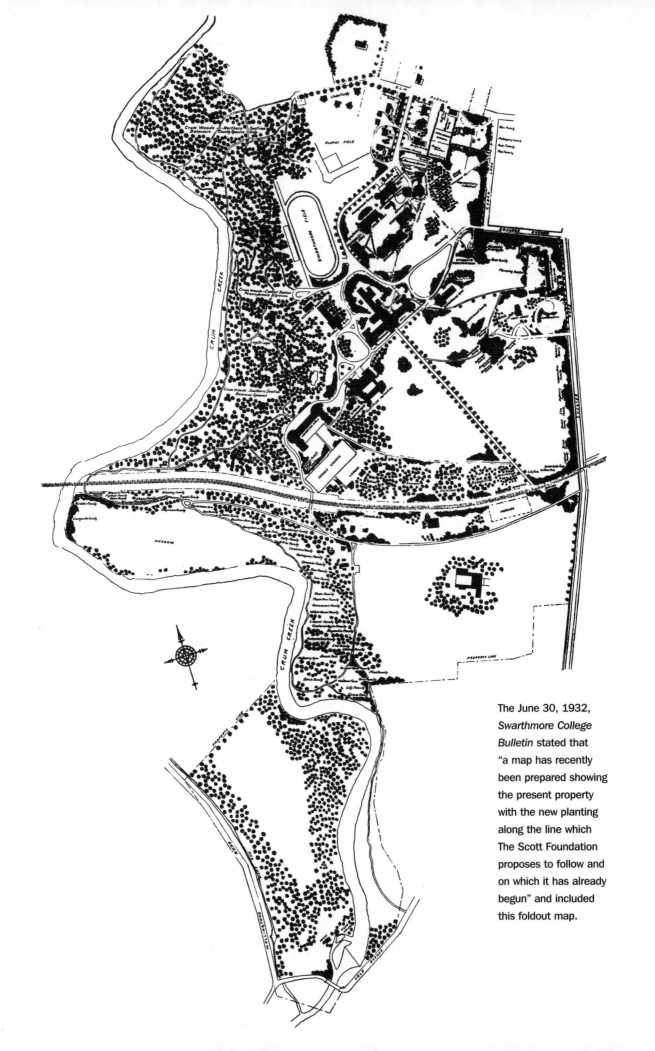

The June 30, 1932, *Swarthmore College Bulletin* stated that "a map has recently been prepared showing the present property with the new planting along the line which The Scott Foundation proposes to follow and on which it has already begun" and included this foldout map.